Notes: (this page intentionally left blank)

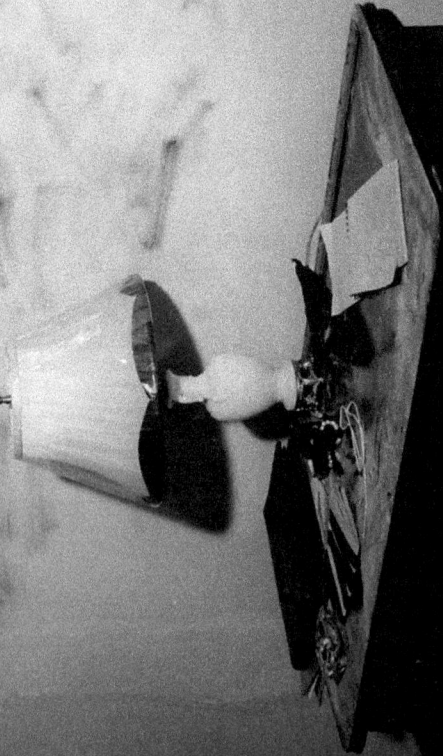

DECRYPTION OF THE LIPSTICK KILLER WALL MESSAGE

First Edition / First Printing

by

Loren L Swearingen

About the front cover:

Original photograph licensed from Corbis Images
This image is also used in the main body of the book

DECRYPTION OF THE LIPSTICK KILLER WALL MESSAGE

First Edition / First Printing
Hard Cover Edition

Loren L Swearingen
Author
United States of America

PREFACE / ACKNOWLEDGEMENTS

The scope of this book is limited to the decryption of the message that was found in Frances Brown's apartment. Other messages attributed to the Lipstick Killer, such as the Suzanne Degnan ransom note and also the lipstick printed sign on the post near the building where the dismembered body of Suzanne Degnan was discovered, are not covered in this book.

Due to the unusual contents and nature of this book, the typical layout and structure found in most conventional books are not being utilized.

The precise terminology used by professional cryptologists is also not being employed in this book.

The book cover photograph of the Lipstick Killer wall message is licensed from Corbis Images. This photograph was also used inside the main body of the book. This photograph is more reliable and accurate than the poor quality image of the Lipstick Killer wall message that often shows up in the internet searches.

References are listed as they are used in the main body of the book.

Some articles from the Chicago Tribune were used as a resource to help provide some basic facts on the Josephine Ross and Frances Brown case.

The following website was used to help decrypt partial anagram segments:
Internet Anagram Server - Wordsmith.org
http://wordsmith.org/anagram/

Licensed copies of Microsoft Office Word and Excel were used to generate the contents of this book.

Google was used as an internet research tool for additional historical information on the Lipstick Killer.

Although the internet is a wonderful research tool, unfortunately, it is also a cyber "place" that is contaminated with much misinformation, disinformation, propaganda, errors, "chat wars", con artists, agendas, misrepresentation of the facts, deliberate distortion of data, trolls, bullies, unreliable reports, slander, unauthorized editing of information, unethical website services, etc. Plus many web sites that are there today are gone tomorrow, in many cases indicative of their "fly-by-night" status.

Hence, with regards to the internet, many times it comes down to a process of data reconciliation, that is, one must deliberate over which data might possibly be valid by comparing them to other data and sources and testing for their validity. But even after this process, often doubts remain with regards to the validity of such data. Hence, the decryption of the Lipstick Killer wall message was used as one of the tools to help determine the validity of some internet data.

THE LIPSTICK KILLER / BRIEF HISTORICAL BACKGROUND

On December 11, 1945, Francis Brown's dead body was discovered alone in her apartment after a cleaning woman heard a radio playing loud and noted Brown's door partly open.

On December 13, 1945, the Chicago Tribune reported that police disclosed the previous night that a Jack-the-Ripper type of slayer was being sought in the murder of a Miss Frances Brown, 33, an attractive secretary / stenographer and former WAVE, who was found shot and stabbed Monday, December 11, 1945, in her sixth-floor apartment, Unit 611, in the Pine Crest Hotel, 3941 Pine Grove Avenue, Chicago, Illinois.

The apartment had been left in shambles, with a bloody trail leading from the victim's blood-soaked bed to her bathroom, where she had been found thrown over the bathtub, with her head resting on the bottom of the bathtub while her legs were outside the bathtub in a kneeling position.

Miss Brown had been savagely stabbed and shot in the head and had a knife lodged in her neck. The knife came from Miss Brown's own kitchen and had been driven in with such force that it had penetrated her neck completely and partially protruded from the other side. Her body had been stripped naked and rinsed of blood, with her neck wrapped in her pajama top and her head wrapped in towels.

Authorities hypothesized that her killer had gotten in by climbing over an eight foot fence and jumping onto the fire escape, but this was never proven beyond a doubt. While police initially believed the murder to have been committed by a burglar who had been interrupted, no valuables had been taken. An "ear-witness", George Weinberg, had heard gunshots at about 4 a.m.

Chief of Detectives Walter G. Storms (*JACK THE RIPPER TYPE SOUGHT AS WAVE'S SLAYER*; Chicago Daily Tribune; Dec 13, 1945; pg. 7) said investigators were impressed by the similarity of Miss Brown's murder to the slaying of another woman within a half mile of the Pine Crest Hotel, Josephine Ross, 43, stabbed in the neck on June 3, 1945, in her apartment at 4108 Kenmore Avenue, Chicago, Illinois.

Josephine Ross's murder, as brutal as it was, did not even make the front pages of the Chicago papers. On the afternoon of June 5, 1945, the dead body of the 43-year-old Josephine Ross was found by her daughter in her mother's home. She had been repeatedly stabbed and her throat was cut. Her wounds had been covered with adhesive tape and her head bound in a skirt. Strangely, the body had then been bathed and a nylon stocking had been wrapped around her neck. The blood-splattered apartment had been left in disarray, but police found no fingerprints and could determine no obvious motive. Reportedly, all that had been stolen from Josephine's apartment was an estimated $12 in cash.

Both Brown and Ross were women without marital ties, had their own apartments, and were stabbed or slashed with knives. A very bizarre commonality was that the slayer washed blood from both of his victims' bodies. No motive had ever been established in the Ross slaying and police likewise were never able to establish a motive in the case of Miss Brown.

Although both victims were murdered in different ways, both women's bodies were mutilated and desecrated after they had died. The killer had taped over the gashes in both victims' bodies with adhesive tape and wrapped an article of clothing around their heads. Another recurring features in these murders was that of bathtubs. Josephine Ross' body was washed in the bathtub in her apartment while Frances Brown's body was washed the same way and was found draped over the edge of the bathtub.

Given the state of forensic science in 1945, police found themselves once more hindered by the lack of evidence in France's Brown apartment. If one assumed that the killer was not wearing gloves at some point, the apartment had apparently been successfully wiped clean of fingerprints. Only one odd bloody fingerprint smudge was found in the apartment according to police. This was a blurred impression apparently from a finger joint. It was discovered near a hinge of the bathroom doorway. Other sources state that the bloody fingerprint smudge was found on the doorjamb of the entrance door.

However, despite this lack of evidence, unlike the murder of Josephine Ross, this time, someone had left a message for the authorities on the living room wall by apparently using Miss Brown's own red lipstick. Later claims that someone other than the killer wrote this message were never supported with any solid evidence.

Chief of Detectives Walter G. Storms (*JACK THE RIPPER TYPE SOUGHT AS WAVE'S SLAYER*; Chicago Daily Tribune; Dec 13, 1945; pg. 7) said the clue that he considered the most important in the murder of Frances Brown is the lipstick writing on the living room wall of Miss Brown's apartment, which read: "For heavens [sic] sake catch me before I kill more I cannot control myself" (photograph of original message from Corbis Images).

In order to create space for this terrifying message, the murderer had removed a picture from the wall, which tended to support the belief that the murderer had executed their crime in a methodical and planned manner.

What was the purpose of this message? Was it a genuine plea for help from a person who could no longer control himself? Did the killer deserve our pity? Or was it a mocking taunt to authorities of more death to come from a sick psychopath who was merely amusing himself by playing a deadly game? What had initially seemed to be just another unfortunate incident in a city -- where crime was not uncommon -- was now beginning to appear to be something very out of the ordinary in a very sinister way. Who was this person? What was his motive? Was anybody and everybody a potential random target of his madness? Where and when would he strike next? Such questions without answers were enough to excite the fears and worries of the public.

Needless to say, this terrifying message was photographed and displayed across newspapers throughout the Chicago area. It was sustenance for

Chicago's sensationalist press and pandered to the insatiable appetite of the public.

This message written in lipstick gave reporters the opportunity to christen the murderer as the "Lipstick Killer", a name which has stuck until this day.

Four days after the murder, the Chicago Police had originally announced they thought that the killer could have possibly been a woman ("*Woman Is Sought As "Lipstick Killer*", Lewiston Daily Sun, December 15, 1945, page 1"). However, upon further investigation and analysis, the police scientific crime detection laboratory indicated that the warning message was probably written by a man.

In 1946, William Heirens was arrested for burglary, interrogated and later formally charged for the murders of Josephine Ross, Frances Brown, and Suzanne Degnan. On September 5, 1946, Chief Justice Harold G. Ward formally sentenced William Heirens to three life terms, which he served until his recent death in 2012 at the age of 83.

But, was William Heirens really the person who wrote the Lipstick Killer wall message?

EXAMINING THE LIPSTICK KILLER WALL CODE

According to a December 13, 1945 article in the Chicago Daily Tribune ("*JACK THE RIPPER TYPE SOUGHT AS WAVE'S SLAYER*", page 7), it states that is was known that Chief of Detectives Walter G. Storms considered the most important clue to be the lipstick message on the wall of Miss Brown's apartment.

According to a December 11, 1945, article in the Chicago Daily Tribune ("*HUNT MAD 'LIPSTICK KILLER'* ", page 1), the lipstick message intrigued police. The writing in itself may be a clue to the killer, they said. The letters were three to six inches high, the highest sentence some six feet from the floor. The phrase, "For heavens [sic] sake" suggested a feminine hand to some detectives, who contended that this expression is more common among women than among men.

However, at a later date, based on further review of the crime scene evidence, the possibility that a woman was the killer was ruled out by the investigators.

Nevertheless, their good observation that this expression, "for heaven's sake", appears at first glance rather odd and somewhat out of place, bears further consideration. After all, if the lipstick writing is taken at face value, then it conveys the message that the killer, after having given in and acted on his strong impulses, and after having committed this heinous murder, is now is a deep state of remorse, and is desperately pleading to the public for help – since he can no longer control himself – by hastily scribbling down his cry for help in a shaky, trembling hand that he can barely control.

The killer, since he needed to escape in a timely manner, could have simply written, "Catch me before I kill more, I cannot control myself", but, he did not. So what value does "for heaven's sake" add to the message? It can be argued that this phrase adds some "awkwardness" to the style of the message. And the detectives were correct in their observation, it is not a common expression used by men, then and now. It could be argued that the expression "for heaven's sake" was being used here as an equivalent

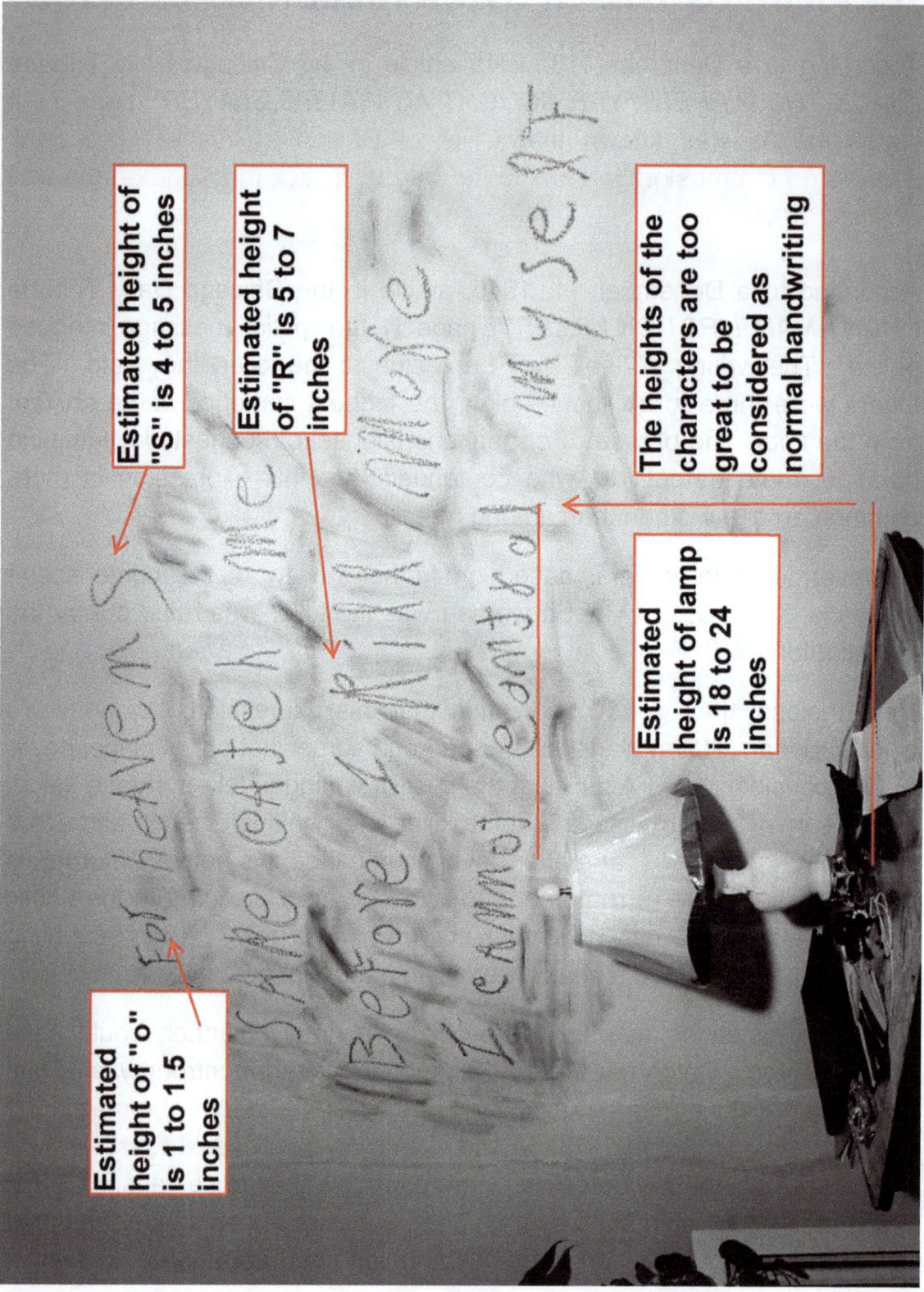

Estimated height of "S" is 4 to 5 inches

Estimated height of "R" is 5 to 7 inches

The heights of the characters are too great to be considered as normal handwriting

Estimated height of "o" is 1 to 1.5 inches

Estimated height of lamp is 18 to 24 inches

for heaven's SAke catch me Before I pRINK Mofe I cannot control myself to, "for God's sake", to show that the killer was asking for people to pray for him so that he could overcome his sinful nature. But, is this really true, especially given the nature of this horrific crime?

But let's suppose this is true, that deep down the killer wants to be caught, and that this written lipstick message is a cry for help and is indicative of his internal struggle with the dark forces inside of him. Why then, does the killer make such an extraordinary effort to disguise his handwriting? In fact, this handwriting is not really even handwriting in the normal sense. Since the characters on the wall were three to six inches high, the normal rote mechanical aspects associated with natural handwriting are now substituted for more of a drawing / painting type of communication. The 56 characters on the wall, which are supposed to represent the letters of the alphabet, are either capital letters or small letters, and, they are either written in cursive or printed. The height of any given letter can vary significantly for apparently no reason. And most importantly, many of the characters are written in such an ambiguous style that these characters could easily be perceive as being a different letter altogether.

To illustrate what is meant by the ambiguity of a written character, it is common in the English language for a "zero", 0, to be confused with the letter "O". It is also common for a small "l" (of the letter "L") to be confused with the number "1" or a capital "I" (capital of "i"). A capital "Q" written in cursive, can be confused with the number "2". The Roman numeral "I" can be confused with a capital "I". However, by historical design, the amount of ambiguity of a written character in the English language (assuming proper penmanship, etc.) is rather small and does not represent a large problem.

However, with the lipstick message, this is not the case. Excluding the three different characters that represent the small letter, "o", as a special case later to be discussed, the lipstick wall message has 28 ambiguous characters out of a total of 56 characters, which means 50% of the characters have an ambiguous style.

Some readers may be understandably a little confused about this talk of ambiguous characters. So, the following examples will illustrate this point:

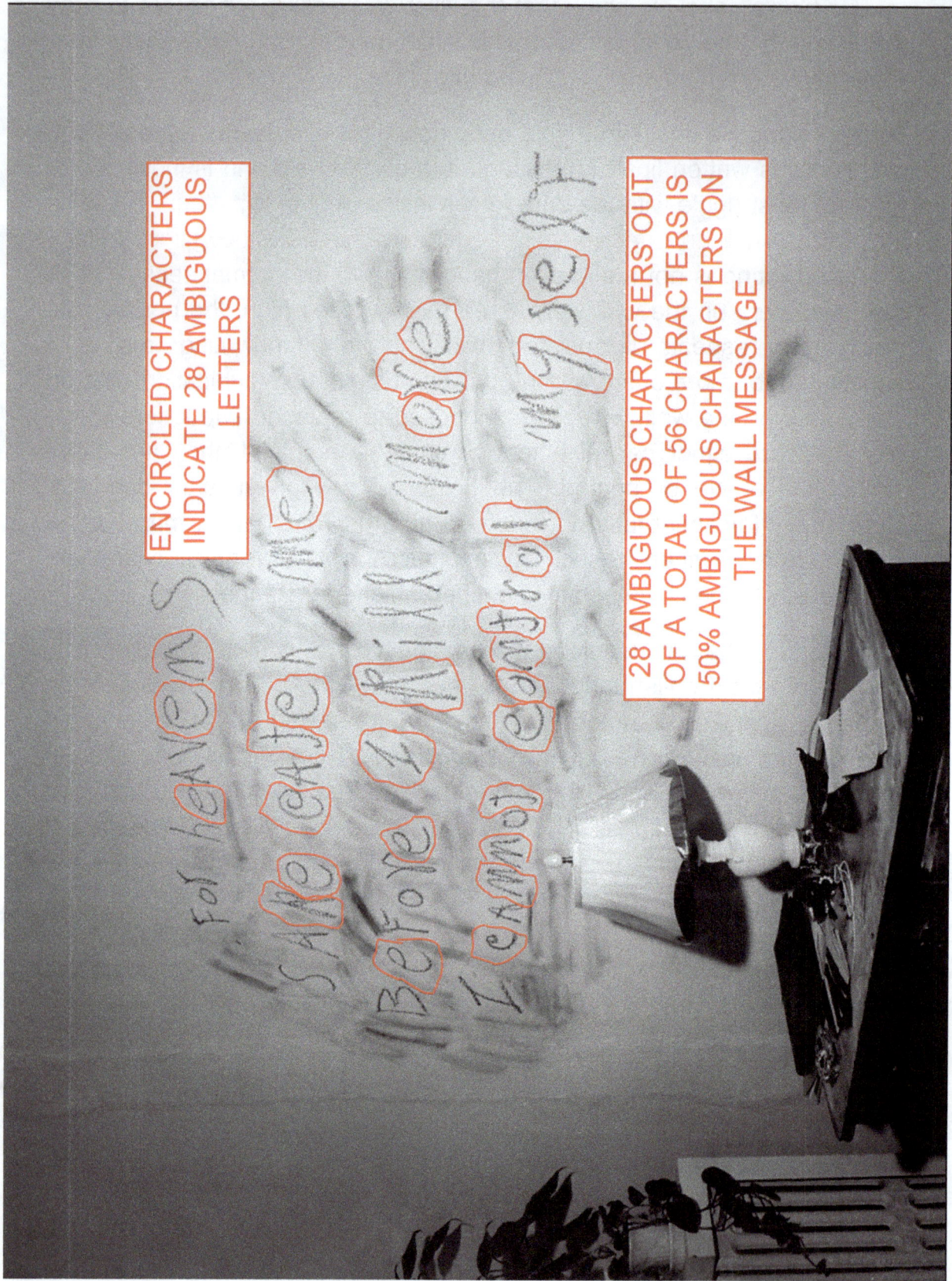

ENCIRCLED CHARACTERS
INDICATE 28 AMBIGUOUS
LETTERS

28 AMBIGUOUS CHARACTERS OUT
OF A TOTAL OF 56 CHARACTERS IS
50% AMBIGUOUS CHARACTERS ON
THE WALL MESSAGE

For heaven s
safe catch me
Before I RIAX more
I cannot control myself

TEST ON WALL MESSAGE READABILITY

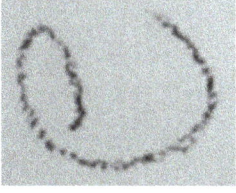

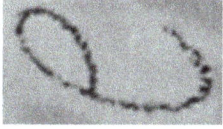

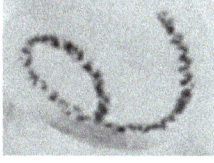

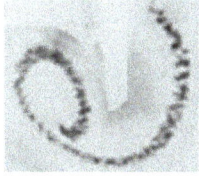

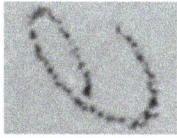

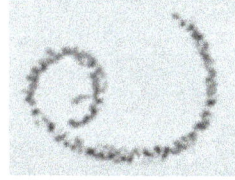

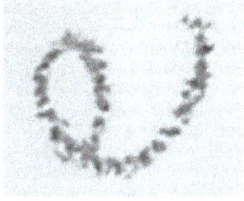

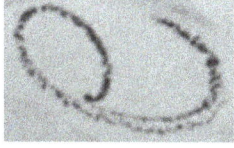

WHICH OF THESE CHARACTERS REPRESENT THE LETTER "C" ?

TEST ON WALL MESSAGE READABILITY

Test On Wall Message Readability

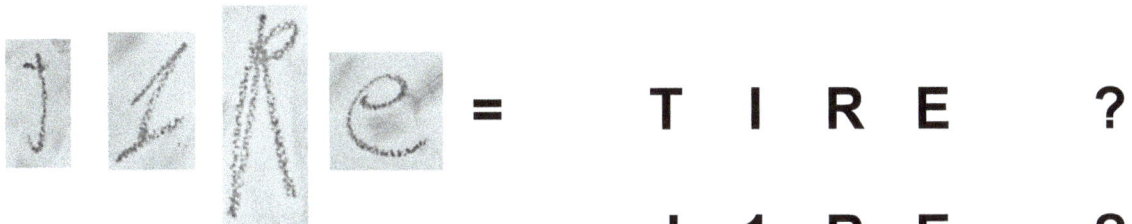 =

T	I	R	E	?
J	1	R	E	?
J	I	R	E	?
T	1	R	E	?

None of the above

Answer According to Wall Message

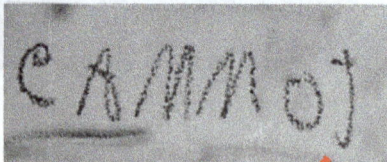

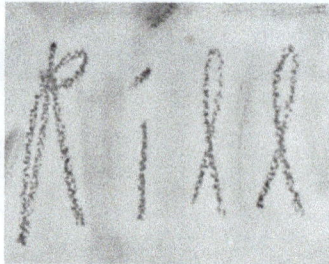

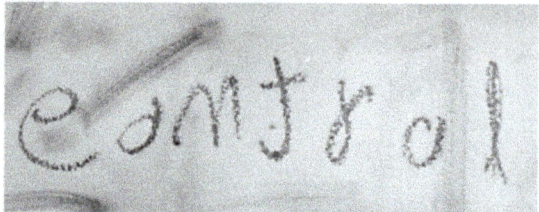

cAMMot I Rill

comtrol

J I K e = **None of the above**

T I K C = **T I K C**

Test On Wall Message Readability

=

J A Y ?

T A R ?

T O Y ?

J O Y ?

J A R ?

T O R ?

None of the above

Answer on other side

T O R = T O R

Test On Wall Message Readability

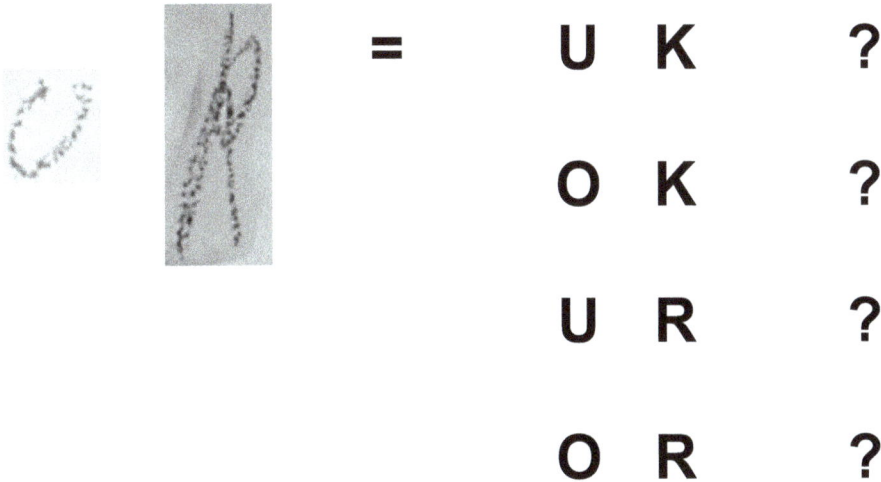 = U K   ?

O K   ?

U R   ?

O R   ?

None of the above

Answer on other side

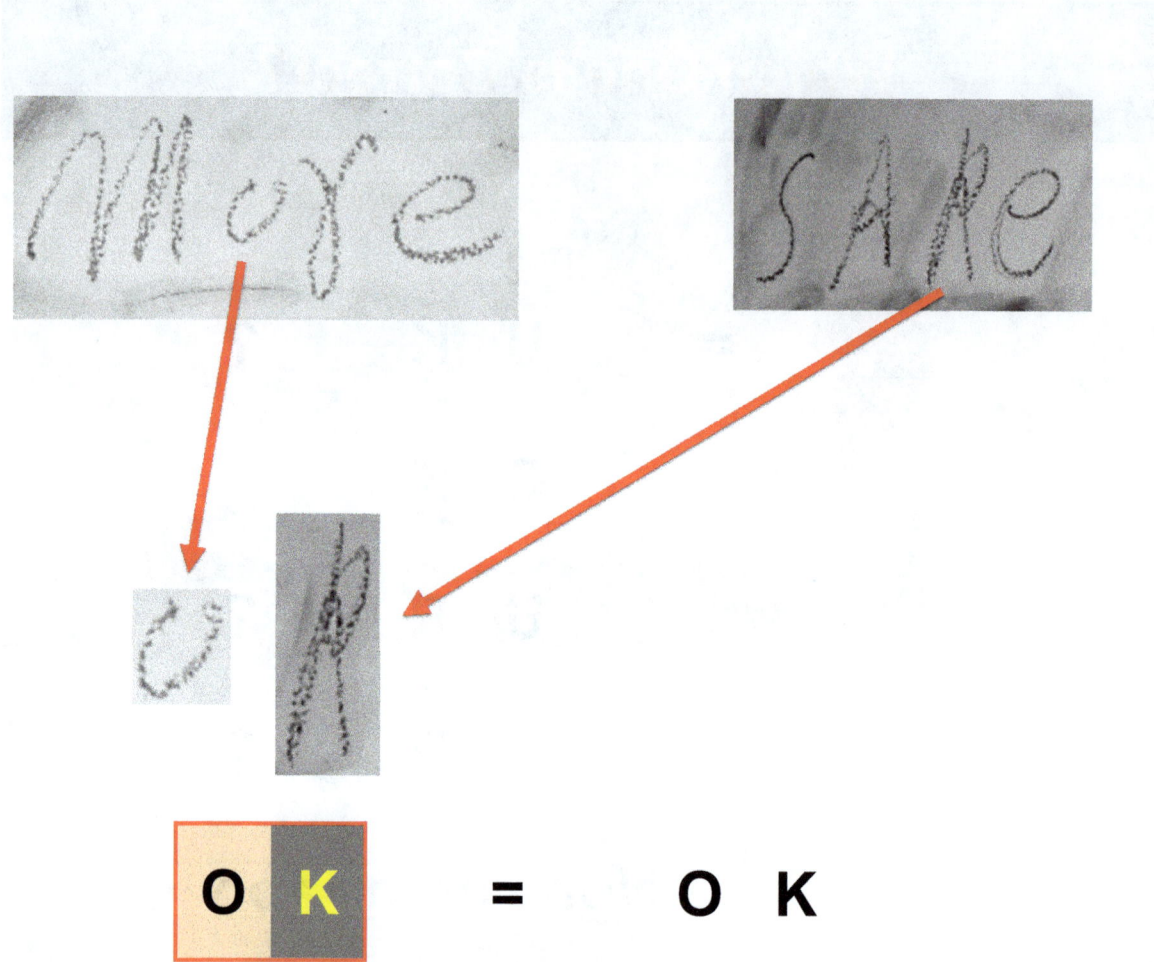

Answer According to Wall Message

O K = O K

Test On Wall Message Readability

=

I	1	C	E	?
L	I	C	E	?
I	I	E	E	?
1	1	C	C	?

None of the above

Answer on other side

Answer According to Wall Message

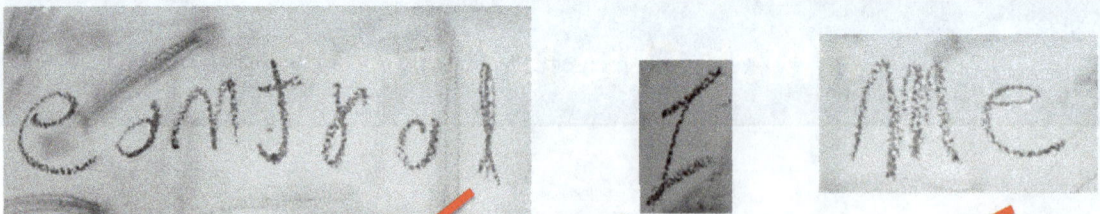

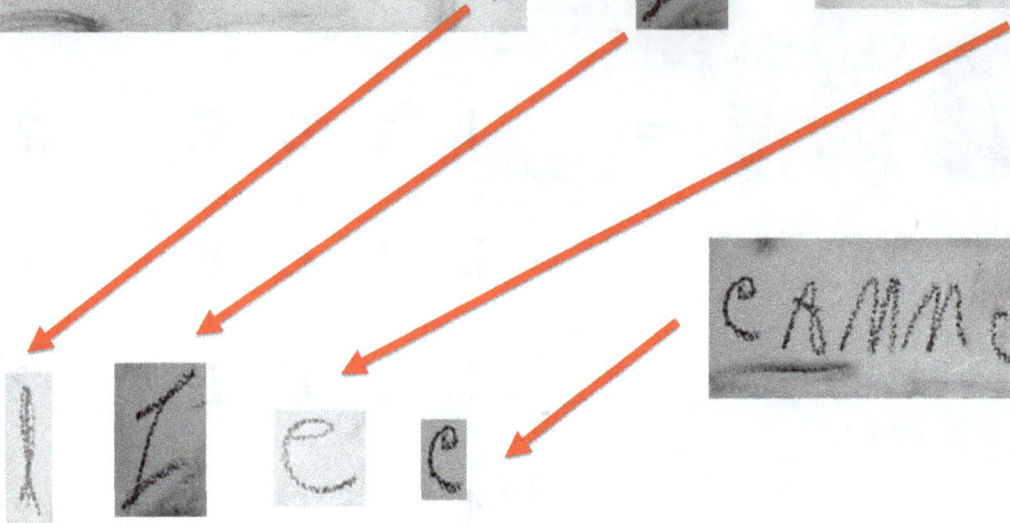

L I E C   =   **None of the above**

Test On Wall Message Readability

$$\mathcal{f}\,\mathit{a}\,\mathit{d} \quad = \quad$$

J	A	D	?
T	O	O	?
T	A	D	?
T	O	D	?
J	O	A	?

Answer on other side

$$T \, O \, O \;\; = \;\; T \, O \, O$$

Test On Wall Message Readability

M i m e =

N	I	M	E	?
N	I	N	E	?
M	L	N	C	?
N	L	N	E	?

None of the above

Answer on other side

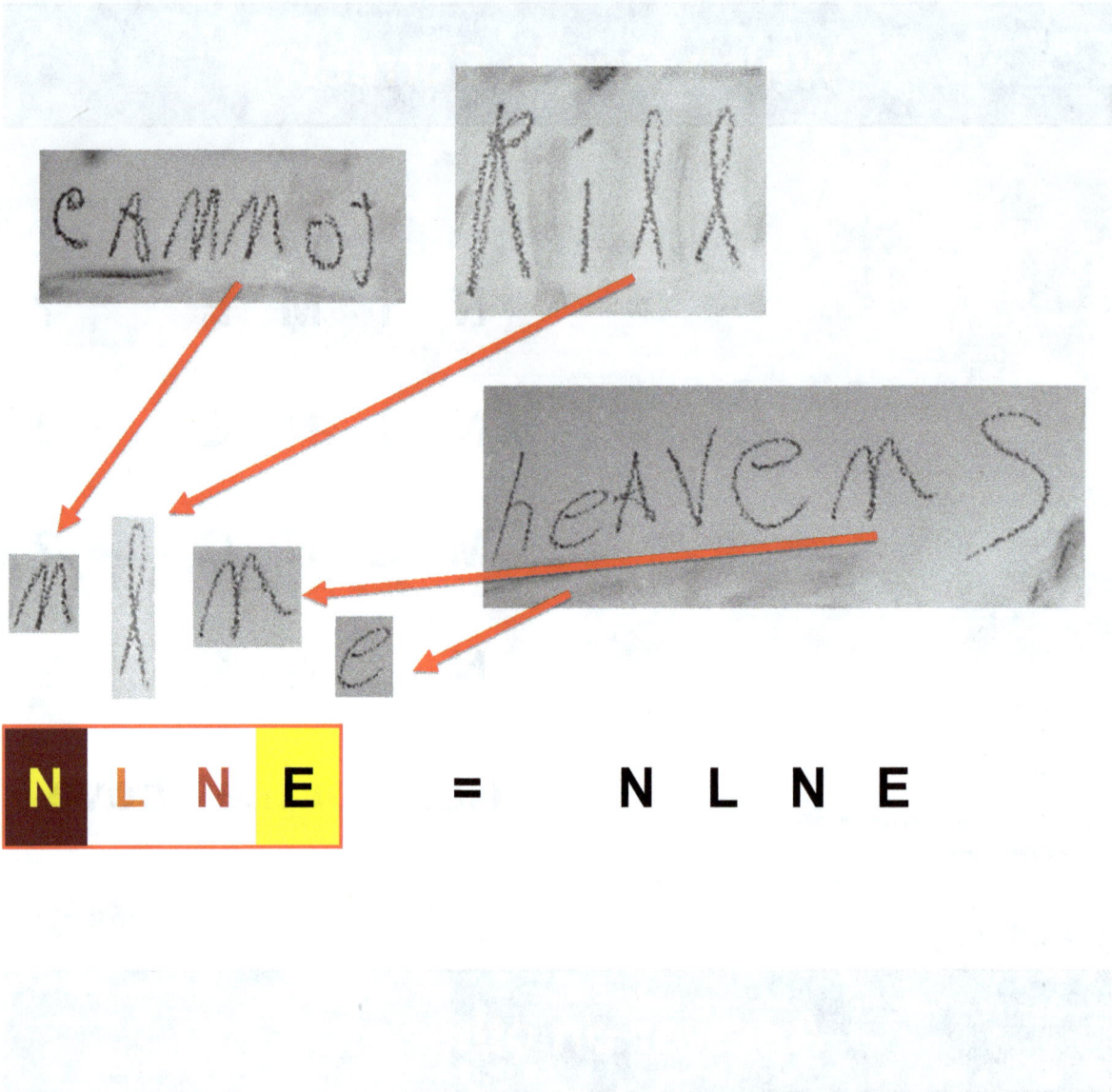

N L N E = N L N E

Test On Wall Message Readability

=

M A R E   ?

M O R E   ?

M A K E   ?

N O R C   ?

N A K E   ?

None of the above

Answer on other side

cAnnot   central   Kill

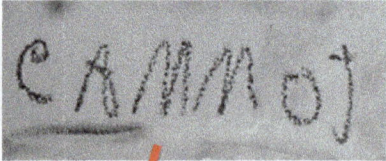

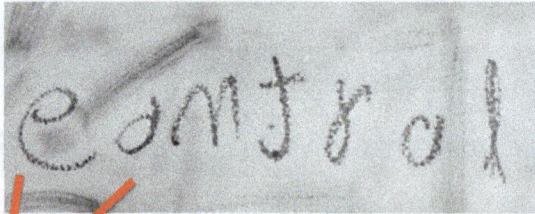

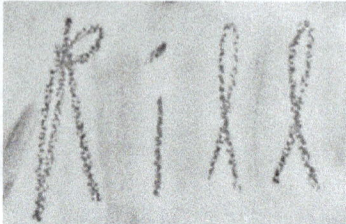

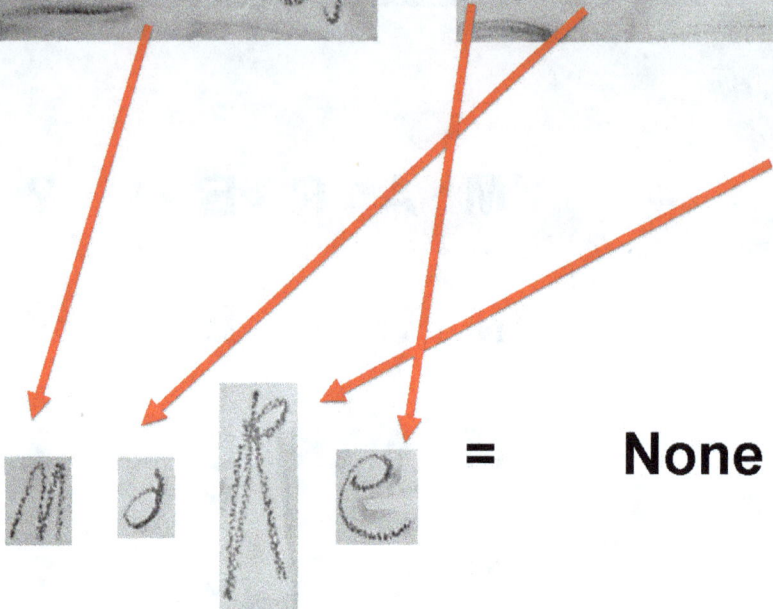

M d K e = **None of the above**

N O K C

So, how did you do on the test? If you made a low test score, do not feel bad, there is nothing wrong with you. That is the way the human brain works (as the originator of the wall message well knew) and that is the way it is supposed to be. To make a long story short, the placement of these ambiguous characters are not a coincidence, they are that way by design and not by accident. But for what reason? Is the killer trying to use this technique to further disguise his natural handwriting? If so, would that not take a lot of premeditation on his part, as opposed to the spontaneity of a despairing maniac (who also needs to escape in a hurry) who supposedly composed and wrote this message in less than a few minutes?

Before we attempt to answer the above questions, and with regards to ambiguous characters, let's look at another strange property of this wall code. There are 12 ambiguous characters that can be used to represent the small letter "e". These 12 characters are 21.4% of the total 56 wall characters, which is significantly higher than the normal letter frequency of the letter "e" in the English language (see appendices). Moreover, these 12 ambiguous characters can represent a transition from a small letter "c" to a small letter "e" as depicted below:

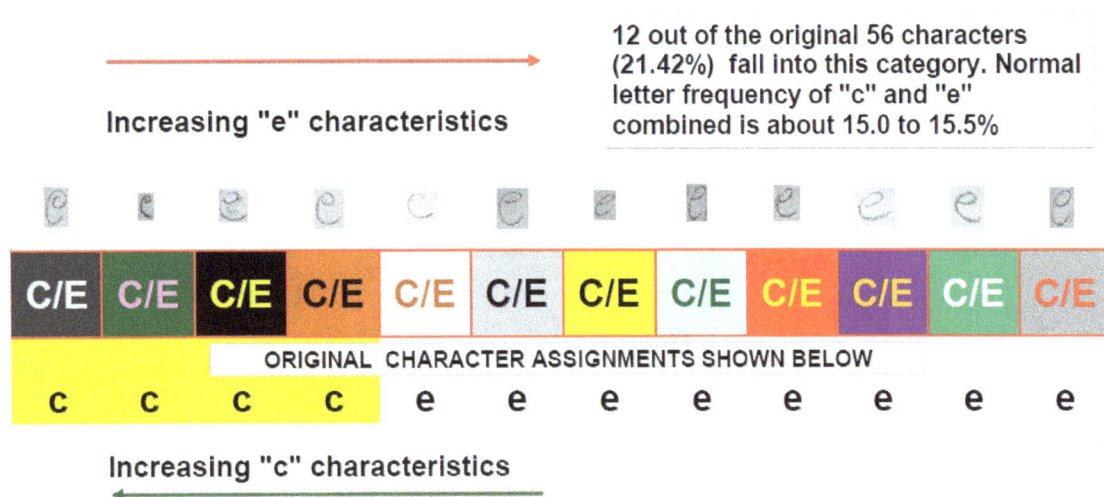

Increasing "e" characteristics

12 out of the original 56 characters (21.42%) fall into this category. Normal letter frequency of "c" and "e" combined is about 15.0 to 15.5%

| C/E | C/E | C/E | C/E | C/E | C/E | C/E | C/E | C/E | C/E | C/E | C/E |

ORIGINAL CHARACTER ASSIGNMENTS SHOWN BELOW

| c | c | c | c | e | e | e | e | e | e | e | e |

Increasing "c" characteristics

At least one "c" and "e" character must be activated to complete decryption

And this "c" to "e" transition is not an exception. What follows are other character transitions that can be found in the wall message:

THE APOSTROPHE IS MISSING FOR "HEAVEN'S"

THERE ARE FOUR LINES TO THIS WALL MESSAGE. JUST LIKE THERE ARE FOUR VERSES IN EACH NOTE.

THESE AMBIGUOUS "E" CHARACTERS ARE THE BASIS FOR CREATING RHYMES IN MOST OF THE REARRANGED NOTES.

ENCIRCLED ARE THE 12 AMBIGUOUS CHARACTERS THAT CAN BE USED TO REPRESENT THE LETTER "E". THESE 12 CHARACTERS ARE 21.4% OF THE TOTAL 56 WALL CHARACTERS, WHICH IS SIGNIFICANTLY HIGHER THAN THE NORMAL LETTER FREQUENCY OF THE LETTER "E" IN THE ENGLISH LANGUAGE.

CHARACTER TRANSITION FROM "c" to "e"

Increasing "e" characteristics →

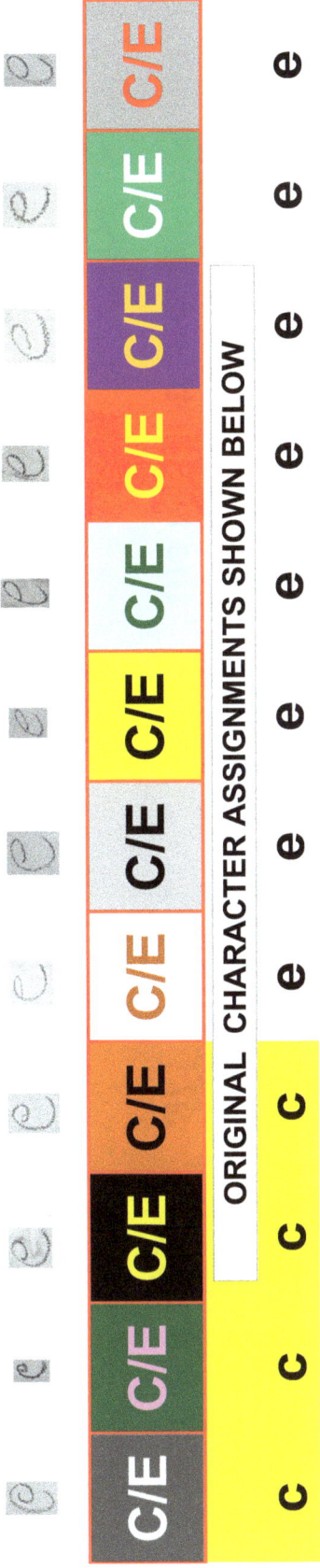

12 out of the original 56 characters (21.42%) fall into this category. Normal letter frequency of "c" and "e" combined is about 15.0 to 15.5%

C/E	C/E	C/E	C/E	C/E	C/E	C/E	C/E	C/E	C/E	C/E	C/E

ORIGINAL CHARACTER ASSIGNMENTS SHOWN BELOW

c	c	c	e	e	e	e	e	e	e	e	e

Increasing "c" characteristics →

At least one "c" and "e" character must be activated to complete decryption

CHARACTER TRANSITION FROM "t" to "j"

High probability

the "j" character is

the first letter of

someone's name

Increasing "j" characteristics

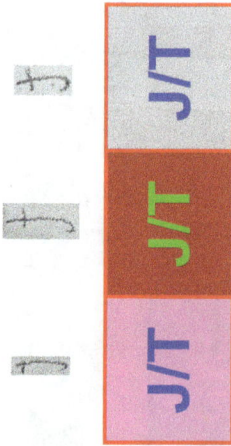

J/T	J/T	J/T

Increasing "t" characteristics

Original message characters are used to represent "t"

At least one "j" character must be activated to complete decryption

CHARACTER TRANSITION FROM "l" to "I"

Increasing "I" characteristics

L/I	L/I	L/I

Increasing "i" characteristics

Original message characters are used to represent "I"

At least one "i" character must be activated to complete decryption

CHARACTER TRANSITION FROM "n" to "m"

Increasing "m" characteristics

N/M	N/M	N/M	N/M

Increasing "n" characteristics

Original message characters are used to represent "n"

At least one "m" character must be activated to complete decryption

CHARACTER TRANSITION FROM "o" to "a" and "d"

Increasing "a" and "d" characteristics

O/A	O/A/ D

Increasing "o" characteristics

Original message characters are used to represent "o"

At least one "a" and "d" character must be activated to complete decryption

CHARACTER TRANSITION FROM "o" to "u"

Increasing "u" characteristics

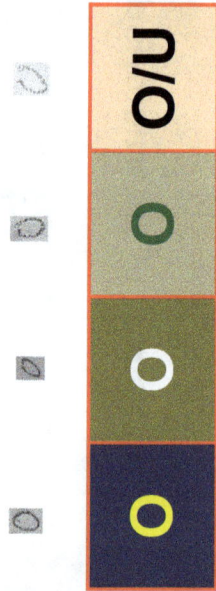

		O/U
O	O	O

Increasing "o" characteristics

Original message characters are used to represent "o"

At least one "u" character must be activated to complete decryption

CHARACTER TRANSITION FROM "r" to "y"

Increasing "y" characteristics

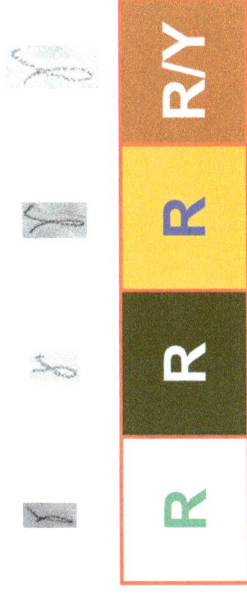

R	R	R	R/Y

Increasing "r" characteristics

Original message characters are used to represent "r"

At least one "y" character must be activated to complete decryption

CHARACTER TRANSITION FROM "O" TO AN ELLIPSIS

This transition

is not in character

ambiguity, but

in perception

Three undersized small "o" letters in a row

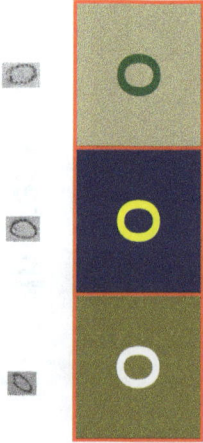

Can be perceived as an ellipsis or small "o" s

Original message characters are used to represent small "o"

At least one ellipsis character must be activated to complete decryption

In the other character transitions that are depicted, the following letters, which are not found in the original message, can be also created: **j, d, u, y** and also an **ellipsis** (triple-dot punctuation mark).

Are these character transitions a coincidence, a figment of a reader's overactive imagination, or do they represent the intent of the originator of the wall message? It can be hypothesized that the purpose of these transitions is to help disguise the purpose of the ambiguous characters and the ambiguous style of the wall messages.

But, before we attempt to answer the above questions, let's look at some other aspects of this wall message.

The characters of the wall message can also be broken down as follows:

- there are 19 capital letters and 37 small letters
- there are 23 printed letters and 33 cursive letters

Once again, are the above simply random characteristics of the 56 characters in an attempt to disguise the wall message so-called handwriting, or, was this an on-purpose design by the murderer of Miss Brown? Or is it both?

Please also note that, despite the supposedly panicked mind of the killer, all of the wall message words are spelled correctly, with the exception of the word "heavens", which is missing a needed apostrophe to make the word "heaven's". Why is the apostrophe missing? It would not take much effort to write it down, so why not write it down?

Also, it should be asked here if the fact that the 13 wall message words are written in four separate lines has any significance, or is this just due to the limitation of available wall space.

Let's now take a closer look at a list of the wall code alphabet, as illustrated on the following pages:

LIPSTICK KILLER WALL MESSAGE - CHARACTERS

#				
1		1/I	=	TWO VALUES - "1" OR "I"
2		A	=	ONE VALUE AS "A"
3		A	=	ONE VALUE AS "A"
4		A	=	ONE VALUE AS "A"
5		A	=	ONE VALUE AS "A"
6		B	=	ONE VALUE AS "B"
7		C/E	=	TWO VALUES - "C" OR "E"
8		C/E	=	TWO VALUES - "C" OR "E"
9		C/E	=	TWO VALUES - "C" OR "E"
10		C/E	=	TWO VALUES - "C" OR "E"
11		C/E	=	TWO VALUES - "C" OR "E"
12		C/E	=	TWO VALUES - "C" OR "E"
13		C/E	=	TWO VALUES - "C" OR "E"

14	*e*	**C/E**	= TWO VALUES - "C" OR "E"
15	*e*	**C/E**	= TWO VALUES - "C" OR "E"
16	*e*	**C/E**	= TWO VALUES - "C" OR "E"
17	*e*	**C/E**	= TWO VALUES - "C" OR "E"
18	*e*	**C/E**	= TWO VALUES - "C" OR "E"
19	*d*	**D/O/A**	= THREE VALUES - "D" OR "O" OR "A"
20	*f*	**F**	= ONE VALUE AS "F"
21	*f*	**F**	= ONE VALUE AS "F"
22	*f*	**F**	= ONE VALUE AS "F"
		G	= NO SYMBOL REPRESENTS "G"
23	*h*	**H**	= ONE VALUE AS "H"
24	*h*	**H**	= ONE VALUE AS "H"
25	*I*	**I**	= ONE VALUE AS "I"

LIPSTICK KILLER WALL MESSAGE - CHARACTERS

26	I/L	= TWO VALUES - "I" OR "L"
27	I	= ONE VALUE AS "I"
28	J/T	= TWO VALUES - "J" OR "T"
29	J/T	= TWO VALUES - "J" OR "T"
30	J/T	= TWO VALUES - "J" OR "T"
31	K/R	= TWO VALUES - "K" OR "R"
32	K/R	= TWO VALUES - "K" OR "R"
33	L/I	= TWO VALUES - "L" OR "I"
34	L/I	= TWO VALUES - "L" OR "I"
35	L/I	= TWO VALUES - "L" OR "I"
36	M	= ONE VALUE AS "M"
37	M	= ONE VALUE AS "M"
38	M	= ONE VALUE AS "M"
39	N/M	= TWO VALUES - "N" OR "M"

40	N/M	=	TWO VALUES - "N" OR "M"
41	N/M	=	TWO VALUES - "N" OR "M"
42	N/M	=	TWO VALUES - "N" OR "M"
43	O	=	ONE VALUE AS "O"
44	O	=	ONE VALUE AS "O"
45	O	=	ONE VALUE AS "O"
46	O/A	=	TWO VALUES - "O" OR "A"
	P	=	NO SYMBOL REPRESENTS "P"
	Q	=	NO SYMBOL REPRESENTS "Q"
47	R	=	ONE VALUE AS "R"
48	R	=	ONE VALUE AS "R"
49	R	=	ONE VALUE AS "R"
50	R/Y	=	TWO VALUES - "R" OR "Y"

LIPSTICK KILLER WALL MESSAGE - CHARACTERS

51		S	=	**ONE VALUE AS "S"**
52		S	=	**ONE VALUE AS "S"**
53		S	=	**ONE VALUE AS "S"**
54		U/O	=	**TWO VALUES - "U" OR "O"**
55		V	=	**ONE VALUE AS "V"**
		W	=	**NO SYMBOL REPRESENTS "W"**
		X	=	**NO SYMBOL REPRESENTS "X"**
56		Y/J	=	**TWO VALUES - "Y" OR "J"**
		Z	=	**NO SYMBOL REPRESENTS "Z"**

It is possible and even probable that the 1945/46 Chicago detectives who worked on this case noticed the same idiosyncrasies of this wall message that we have discussed here and suspected the possibility that the wall message might be an encrypted message. They would then have assigned the task of decryption to experienced code breakers, maybe even using federal resources. These code breakers would have tried a variety of decryption methods, both simple and complex. In many cases, they would have tried to use or look for an obvious keyword like "Frances Brown" or even "Josephine Alice Ross", whose murder highly resembled the murder of Frances Brown. However, using these keywords (for certain type of decryption methods where they would be needed) would not have worked since the wall code alphabet does not contain the letter "w", and hence, can never spell the victim's name of Frances Brown. There is also no "p" in the wall code alphabet for spelling "Josephine Ross". Hence, these would-be-code breakers would eventually give up and report to their supervisors that the lipstick wall message was not encrypted. And there probably would not have been any good reason to have these failed, decryption attempts published in the local daily Chicago newspapers.

On the other hand, the originator of the lipstick wall message, may have been, and probably was, smart enough to realize, that if he did place a "w" and a "p" in his alphabet, and if the names of "Frances Brown" and "Josephine Ross" were indeed used as obvious keywords, then this would be the first thing that the code breakers would try – and having then succeeded at breaking the code – the killer could then have been in significant danger of being identified and caught.

But if the lipstick killer wall message is encrypted, how is it done? How did the killer fool the experts? What did the experts miss? If the wall message is encrypted, is it even possible to break?

Let's go back and look at the ambiguous "e" characters that were earlier discussed and see what purpose they could possibly serve. If needed, they can be the basis for allowing the flexible creation of rhymes whenever the 56 characters of the original note are rearranged within the note to create a new note with a new message. This rearrangement of characters is similar to an anagram, but significantly differs in that the values of the characters (as letters) being re-arranged can also change, thus making the arrival of a solution much more difficult. The hypothesized, imposed constraint to rhyme, if true, would help provide structure to the decrypted message and help decrypt the message.

Using the website, Internet Anagram Server, http://wordsmith.org/anagram/ and after many trial-and-error attempts, the following decrypted first page was generated (see the larger version of the following for better viewing):

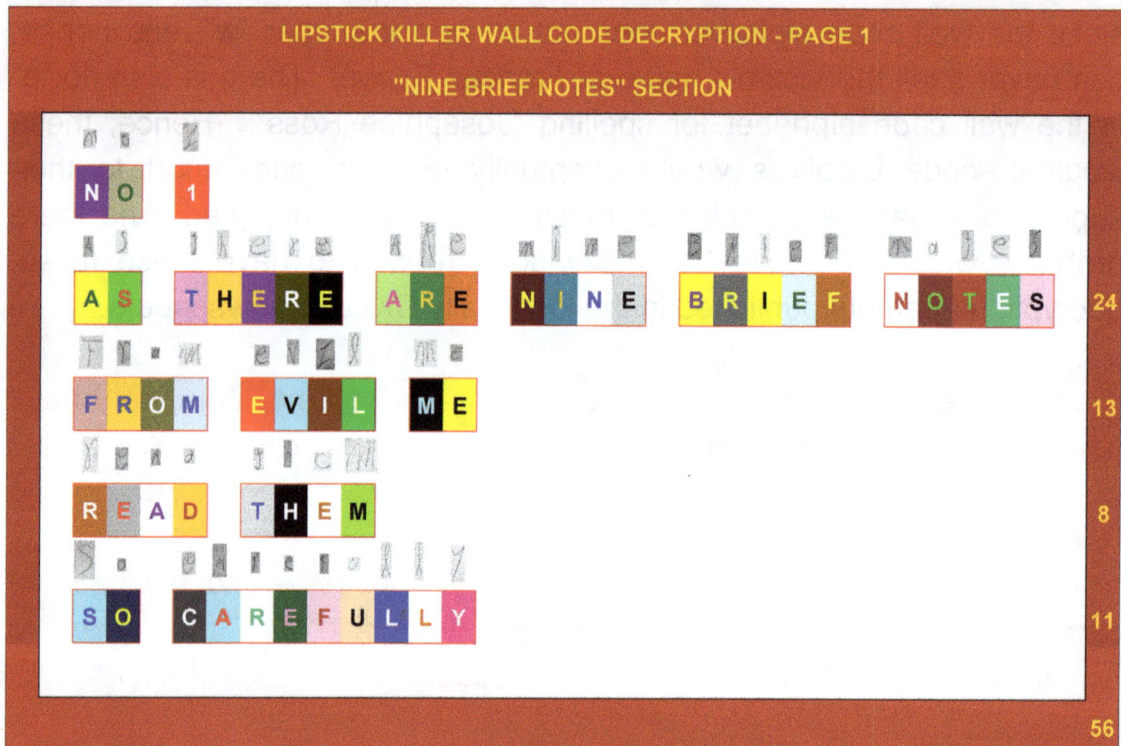

LIPSTICK KILLER WALL CODE DECRYPTION - PAGE 1

"NINE BRIEF NOTES" SECTION

NO 1

AS THERE ARE NINE BRIEF NOTES 24

FROM EVIL ME 13

READ THEM 8

SO CAREFULLY 11

56

Hence, the above is a plausible starting point that will later need some type of internal confirmation as to correctness from the very same decrypted message. Here we can see the first use of the ambiguous "e" to help the message flow smoothly and rhyme. The skeptic here will understandably see the above as a "force-fit" solution. The skeptic's questions will be answered here in due time as more notes become decrypted.

Using the same techniques as described above, the following decrypted second page was generated:

LIPSTICK KILLER WALL CODE DECRYPTION - PAGE 2

"NINE BRIEF NOTES" SECTION

FOUR VERSES IN NOTE   16

MAKE FINAL LINE RHYME   18

EACH TO BEAR   10

TALES OF CRIME   12

56

Here we can again see the use of the ambiguous "e" to help the message flow smoothly and to rhyme. Also, this second page, which contains important instructional information, is consistent with and confirms to some minor degree how the first page was generated.

So what we have thus far is that the first two pages of the nine brief notes are instructional with regards to solving all nine notes. Even given the flexible nature of a poem, all words are spelled correctly here and there are no grammatical mistakes. Hence, the skeptic cannot complain about "force-fitting" with regards to using misspelled words or forcing poor grammar in order to arrive at a pre-ordained conclusion.

16
18
10
12
56

NOTE

RHYME

IN

LINE

VERSES

FINAL

BEAR

CRIME

TO

OF

FOUR

MAKE

EACH

TALES

So, given that the first two pages out of nine provide instructional information with regards to decrypting the lipstick killer wall code, the remaining seven message probably contain the "meat" of the main message.

Thus far, one of the rejected words from the previous many trial-and-error attempts was an interesting word -- the word "reference" -- a nine letter word out of 56 available letters, hence, not something that is easy to form given the constraints. Then we also have the ambiguous "I" that can also be interpreted as a "1". So who would be a "reference 1" that the killer could brag about? Would it not be Josephine Alice Ross? So, let's try it:

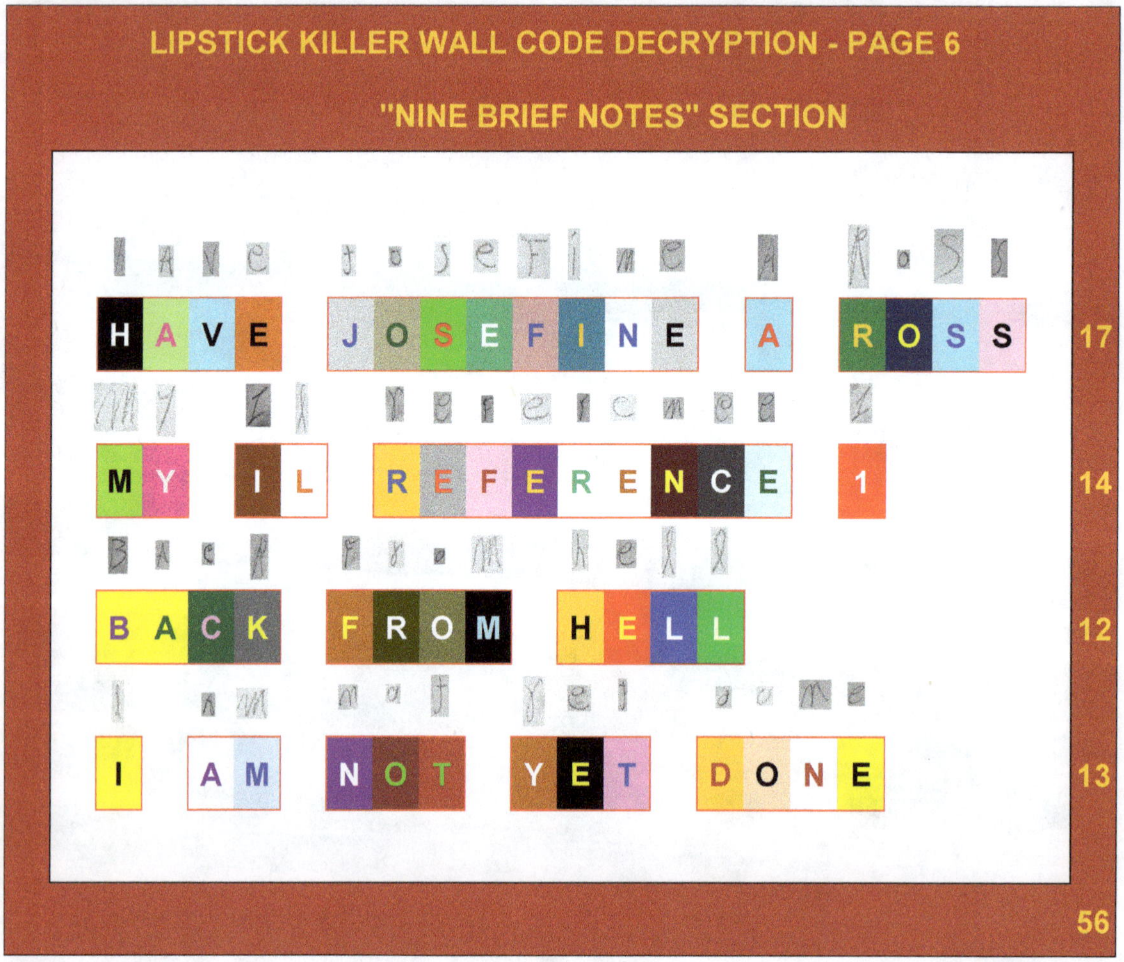

LIPSTICK KILLER WALL CODE DECRYPTION - PAGE 6
"NINE BRIEF NOTES" SECTION
HAVE JOSEFINE A ROSS 17
MY IL REFERENCE 1 14
BACK FROM HELL 12
I AM NOT YET DONE 13
56

Here at long last, is a voluntary written confirmation of what Chicago detectives had long suspected.

Also note here that the killer says "Illinois reference 1", not just "reference 1", suggesting that he had probably killed at least one person outside of Illinois before he murdered Josephine Ross.

In addition, this rules out the killer's involvement with the violent murder of a Miss Estelle Carey, 34, whose throat was slashed February 1943 in her apartment at 512 Addison Street in Chicago. Chief of Detectives Walter G. Storms said that investigators had been impressed with the similarity between the murder of Miss Brown, Josephine Ross and Estelle Carey during the last two and one-half years within a half mile of the Pine Crest (*JACK THE RIPPER TYPE SOUGHT AS WAVE'S SLAYER;* Chicago Daily Tribune; Dec 13, 1945; pg. 7). This decrypted note generates some new information, albeit minor in nature, and is not simply a regurgitation of what is already known or suspected.

But what about the misspelling of "Josephine" as "Josefine"? Isn't that force-fitting? No, on the contrary. First, the two are phonetically identical in the English language. Secondly, the decrypted message has no "awkwardness" to it and "flows very smooth" and is accurate in the description of the killer as "being back from hell" and "not yet done". And most importantly, as previously discussed, but worth repeating here:

The originator of the lipstick wall message, may have been, and probably was, smart enough to realize, that if he did place a "w" and a "p" in his alphabet, and if the names of "Frances Brown" and "Josephine Ross" were indeed used as obvious keywords, then this would be the first thing that the code breakers would try – and having then succeeded at breaking the code – the killer could then have been in significant danger of being identified and caught.

The killer gets around this by using phonetically equivalent spellings of the victim's names, which we will see again in the next decrypted note.

AT FRANCES BROUN 14

I CLEARLY SEE 11

KNIFE FROM NECK SHOT TO HEAD 23

IM EVIL ME 8

56

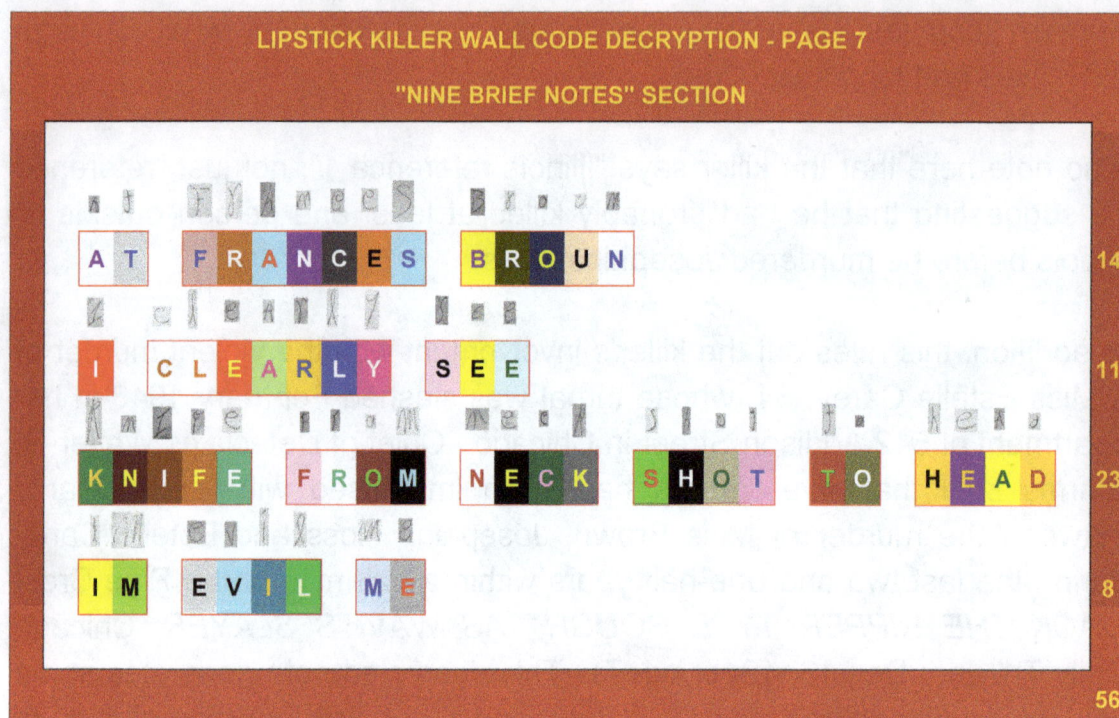

Here we can again see the use of the ambiguous "e" to help the message flow smoothly and to rhyme.

The name of "Broun" is again a phonetically equivalent spelling of "Brown" and the description of the inflicted injuries to the victim are consistent with newspaper accounts. Notice here that the decrypted message accurately states, "Knife from neck", instead of the more common, "Knife to neck".

One can deduce from this decrypted note, since it was created before the murder of Miss Brown took place, that the killer planned this type of particular overall injury in order to satisfy the requirements of the encrypted message, and also to convince future code breakers than this particular murder and wall message were all pre-mediated and well planned.

The skeptics here will understandably state that this decrypted message is simply echoing back what the author of this book read in the newspapers, hence, this is a "force-fit" and not a valid solution. While it is true that the author of this book did due diligence to read the newspapers for the background of this particular murder, the skeptics do not realize that this

LIPSTICK KILLER WALL CODE DECRYPTION - PAGE 7

"NINE BRIEF NOTES" SECTION

AT FRANCES BROUN	14
I CLEARLY SEE	11
KNIFE FROM NECK SHOT TO HEAD	23
IM EVIL ME	8
	56

solution was obtained only after very many computer aided trial-and-error attempts in which no alternative solution was determined to be competitive. Hence, for this particular decrypted message to coincide with the historical facts of the murder does not necessitate that it is somehow an invalid solution and that it is somehow concrete proof of "force-fitting" a solution.

Thus far the killer has talked about who he has killed in the past in Illinois (Josephine Alice Ross) and who he has presently killed in Illinois (Frances Brown). Does he talk about any potential future victims? Let's see:

LIPSTICK KILLER WALL CODE DECRYPTION - PAGE 8

"NINE BRIEF NOTES" SECTION

HEREOF ILL MAKE 13

YES FEAR TO SEE 12

FROM A SMALL ONE 13

A VICTIM NUMBER THREE 18

56

Once again, this decrypted note is a voluntary written confirmation of what Chicago detectives will suspect in the future -- the connection between the murder of Frances Brown and the future murder of Suzanne Degnan.

"NINE BRIEF NOTES" SECTION

MAKE

SEE

ONE

THREE

ILL

TO

NUMBER

HEREOF

SMALL

FEAR

A

VICTIM

YES

FROM

A

13

12

13

18

56

The skeptics will again argue that the use of the ambiguous "e" to help the message flow smoothly and to rhyme is used as a tool to force-fit a solution that obviously refers to Suzanne Degnan's future gruesome murder in early 1946 in Chicago. Once again, for this particular decrypted message to coincide with the historical facts does not necessitate that it is somehow an invalid solution and that it is somehow concrete proof of "force-fitting" a solution. It is interesting, albeit sad, to note that if this lipstick wall message could have been decrypted to this point, perhaps city authorities could have warned the local residents to be on a special alert for this type of sick predator.

Others will argue that the word, "I'll", used in this particular decrypted note cannot be used here since it is misspelled – being that an apostrophe was not used to correctly spell the word. However, the original lipstick wall message uses the expression "for heavens sake" without an apostrophe before the "s" in "heavens" (hence, it is misspelled), yet the skeptics have no problem in accepting the valid content of the original message. The obvious rule here is – set by the originator of the lipstick wall message – is that apostrophes are not available from the original message and are not needed, that is, they are not considered and are not important. The originator of the lipstick wall message had good reason to not include an apostrophe in the original message. If he had, it would be extremely difficult, if not impossible, to have a multi-note decrypted message since an apostrophe would have to be included in every decrypted note. Nevertheless, the killer thought it was important enough to include the phrase "for heavens sake".

Thus far we have decrypted five of the nine notes. But nothing that has been learned or confirmed so far has led us any closer to posthumously identifying the killer. So why would the killer write the lipstick message in the first place? Would he do it to state the obvious? That is, that he has killed Frances Brown, as any investigator can plainly see? No, the main reason he has written the message is because he has indeed encrypted his name inside the wall message. That is what makes it exciting for him – he wants to prove that he is far more intelligent than his adversaries.

But how will the killer reveal his name inside one of the remaining encrypted notes? What technique will he use since a very large number of names can be generated from the 56 character code? To illustrate this problem, consider the following invalid force-fitted decryption:

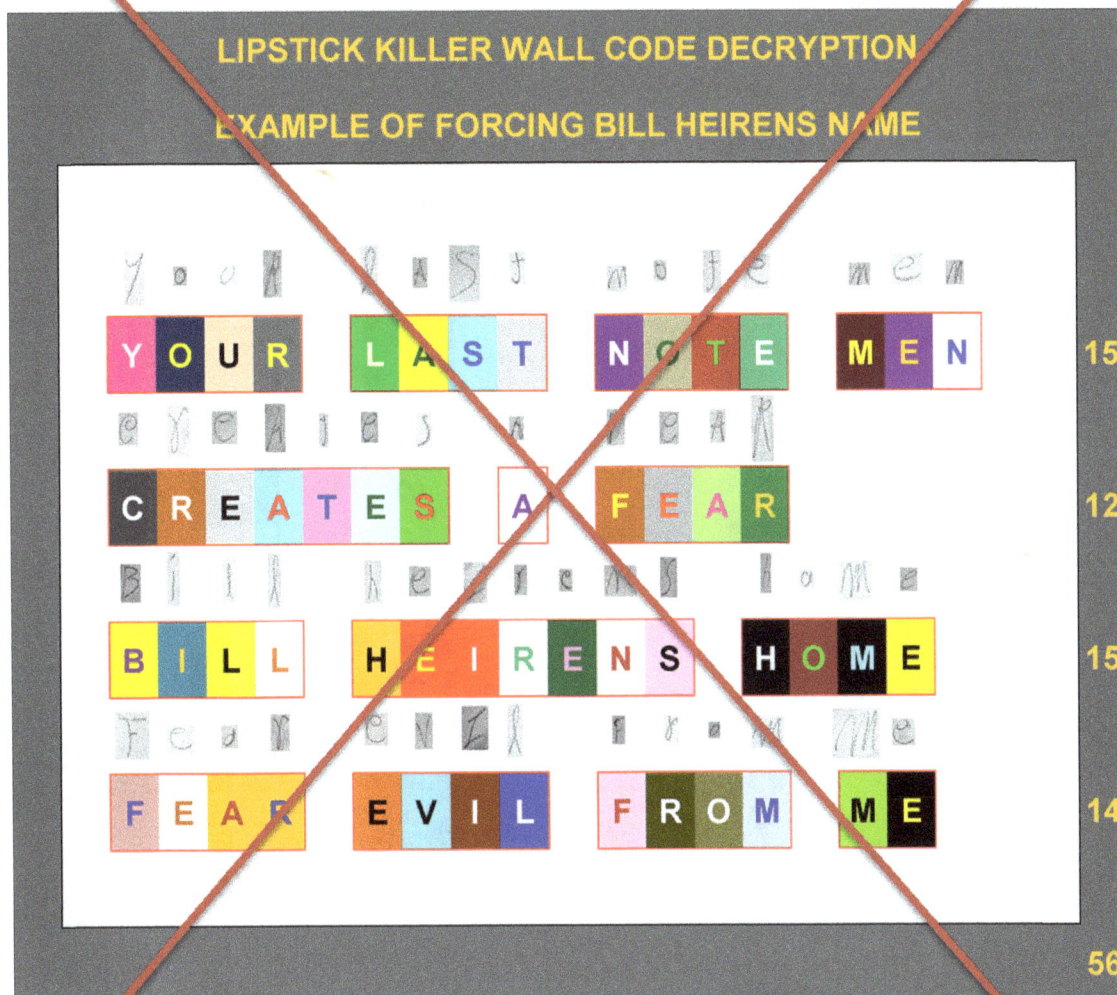

LIPSTICK KILLER WALL CODE DECRYPTION

EXAMPLE OF FORCING BILL HEIRENS NAME

| YOUR | LAST | NOTE | MEN | 15 |

| CREATES | A | FEAR | | 12 |

| BILL | HEIRENS | HOME | | 15 |

| FEAR | EVIL | FROM | ME | 14 |

| | | | | 56 |

Even though this particular invalid decrypted note does not rhyme (and is also a good example of an awkward, force-fit solution), given time and effort; a decryption that *does* rhyme and also includes Bill Heirens name could eventually be found. Does this mean that Bill Heirens is the Lipstick Killer? This same logic could also be applied to many, many other names. So how does the originator of the wall message overcome this problem? He does so by using several tools. Let's look at the first one:

LIPSTICK KILLER WALL CODE DECRYPTION

EXAMPLE OF FORCING BILL HEIRENS NAME

15

12

15

14

56

YOUR LAST NOTE MEN

CREATES A FEAR HOME

BILL HEIRENS EVIL FROM

FEAR ME

LOOK OFF NOTES — 12

FROM MY ADVICE — 12

THE MAN A KILLER BE — 15

SEE NAME RISE THRICE — 17

56

So here the originator of the lipstick message establishes that the killer's name must show up three times in the remaining three encrypted notes. And he has also previously given us a possible hint at the killer's initials:

Increasing "j" characteristics

J/T   J/T   J/T

Increasing "t" characteristics

High probability the "j" character is the first letter of someone's name

LIPSTICK KILLER WALL CODE DECRYPTION - PAGE 3

"NINE BRIEF NOTES" SECTION

LOOK OFF NOTES

FROM MY ADVICE

THE MAN A KILLER BE

SEE NAME RISE THRICE

That is, the letter "J" is needed as the first letter of someone's name. We have already used this letter "J" for Josephine Ross' name in one of the earlier decrypted notes, but, if you think about it, she could have easily been identified as simply Miss Ross, since all concerned would have readily known that it was a reference to Josephine Ross. Hence, this extra encryption effort to generate a "J" was not absolutely needed for Josephine Ross' name, but was absolutely needed for the killer's name. Therefore, one of the initials of the killer is a "J" in all likelihood. And there is even some possibility that the other initial of the killer is a "T" since that is the original letter from which the letter "J" emerges.

So let's try the following: one remaining decrypted note for the first name, the second for the surname, and then the last note for the whole name:

LIPSTICK KILLER WALL CODE DECRYPTION - PAGE 4

"NINE BRIEF NOTES" SECTION

MY 1ST NAME IS

11

The preceding partially, potentially decrypted message is what we have so far with regards to generating a first name for the killer. So now what do we do?

It is possible that past would-be code breakers got this far, but had to give up at this point since the list of potential first names is extremely high.

So, let's look inside our tool box of decryption tools for some more help.

The first decryption tool is a very simple one, that is, according to the Chicago investigators (*JACK THE RIPPER TYPE SOUGHT AS WAVE'S SLAYER;* Chicago Daily Tribune; Dec 13, 1945; pg. 7), the collected evidence pointed to the fact that the killer is a man, thus, female first names can be eliminated.

The second decryption tool is also a very simple one, that is, the killer's native tongue is more than likely to be American English. Hence, his first and last names are going to probably be not too difficult to spell or pronounce in American English, including the possibility that his surname has been anglicized.

Also, as a reminder, remember that the following letters are not available in the lipstick wall message alphabet, and hence, cannot be used to create a first or last name:

G, P, Q, W, X and Z

Again, as a reminder, as previously discussed, since one of the killer's initials must have the letter "J", then it is possible that the first name of the killer could start with the letter "J".

So what other decryption tools do we have?

Let's now take a closer look at the list of capital letters and small letters of the wall code alphabet, as indicated on the following pages:

For heAvenS
SAke cAtch Me
BeFore I Kill More
I cAnnot control MySelF
ENCIRCLED CHARACTERS
INDICATE THE 19 CAPITAL
LETTERS ON THE WALL MESSAGE

LIPSTICK KILLER WALL MESSAGE - CHARACTERS AS CAPITAL LETTERS

#	Character		Activation
1	1/I	=	ACTIVATED BY THE WORD "REFERENCE 1"
2	A	=	ACTIVATED AS FIRST WORD IN SENTENCE
3	A	=	ACTIVATED AS FIRST WORD IN SENTENCE
4	A	=	ACTIVATED AS FIRST WORD IN SENTENCE
5	A	=	ACTIVATED BY THE INITIAL "A" for JOSEPHINE ALICE ROSS
6	B	=	ACTIVATED BY THE WORD "BROWN"
7	C/E	=	ACTIVATED BY THE WORD "CALIFORNIA"
8	F	=	ACTIVATED BY THE WORD "FRANCES"
9	F	=	ACTIVATED BY THE WORD "FRANCISCO"
10	F	=	ACTIVATED BY THE WORD "FLOVA"

LIPSTICK KILLER WALL MESSAGE - CHARACTERS AS CAPITAL LETTERS

#	Letter		Activation
11	**I**	=	ACTIVATED BY THE WORD "I" OR "IL"
12	**K/R**	=	ACTIVATED BY THE INITIAL "R" for JOSEPHINE ALICE ROSS
13	**M**	=	ACTIVATED BY THE WORD "MR"
14	**M**	=	ACTIVATED BY THE WORD "MS"
15	**M**	=	ACTIVATED BY THE WORD "MOTHER"
16	**S**	=	ACTIVATED BY THE INITIALS "SF"
17	**S**	=	ACTIVATED BY THE WORD "SAN FRANCISCO"
18	**S**	=	ACTIVATED BY THE INITIALS "S 1 C"
19	**Y/J**	=	ACTIVATED BY THE WORD "JACK"

#		Color		Value
1		C/E	=	TWO VALUES - "C" OR "E"
2		C/E	=	TWO VALUES - "C" OR "E"
3		C/E	=	TWO VALUES - "C" OR "E"
4		C/E	=	TWO VALUES - "C" OR "E"
5		C/E	=	TWO VALUES - "C" OR "E"
6		C/E	=	TWO VALUES - "C" OR "E"
7		C/E	=	TWO VALUES - "C" OR "E"
8		C/E	=	TWO VALUES - "C" OR "E"
9		C/E	=	TWO VALUES - "C" OR "E"
10		C/E	=	TWO VALUES - "C" OR "E"

LIPSTICK KILLER WALL MESSAGE - CHARACTERS AS SMALL LETTERS

#		Character		Value
11		C/E	=	TWO VALUES - "C" OR "E"
12		D/O/A	=	THREE VALUES - "D" OR "O" OR "A"
13		H	=	ONE VALUE AS "H"
14		H	=	ONE VALUE AS "H"
15		I/L	=	TWO VALUES - "I" OR "L"
16		I	=	ONE VALUE AS "I"
17		J/T	=	TWO VALUES - "J" OR "T"
18		J/T	=	TWO VALUES - "J" OR "T"
19		J/T	=	TWO VALUES - "J" OR "T"
20		K/R	=	TWO VALUES - "K" OR "R"

LIPSTICK KILLER WALL MESSAGE - CHARACTERS AS SMALL LETTERS

#	Character		Value
21	L/I	=	TWO VALUES - "L" OR "I"
22	L/I	=	TWO VALUES - "L" OR "I"
23	L/I	=	TWO VALUES - "L" OR "I"
24	N/M	=	TWO VALUES - "N" OR "M"
25	N/M	=	TWO VALUES - "N" OR "M"
26	N/M	=	TWO VALUES - "N" OR "M"
27	N/M	=	TWO VALUES - "N" OR "M"
28	O	=	ONE VALUE AS "O"
29	O	=	ONE VALUE AS "O"
30	O	=	ONE VALUE AS "O"

LIPSTICK KILLER WALL MESSAGE - CHARACTERS AS SMALL LETTERS

No.	Character	Decode
31	O/A	= TWO VALUES - "O" OR "A"
32	R	= ONE VALUE AS "R"
33	R	= ONE VALUE AS "R"
34	R	= ONE VALUE AS "R"
35	R/Y	= TWO VALUES - "R" OR "Y"
36	U/O	= TWO VALUES - A "U" OR "O"
37	V	= ONE VALUE AS "V"

What if we take the list of the 19 capital letters only and form a cross-word puzzle? The only reasonable solution that was found is as follows:

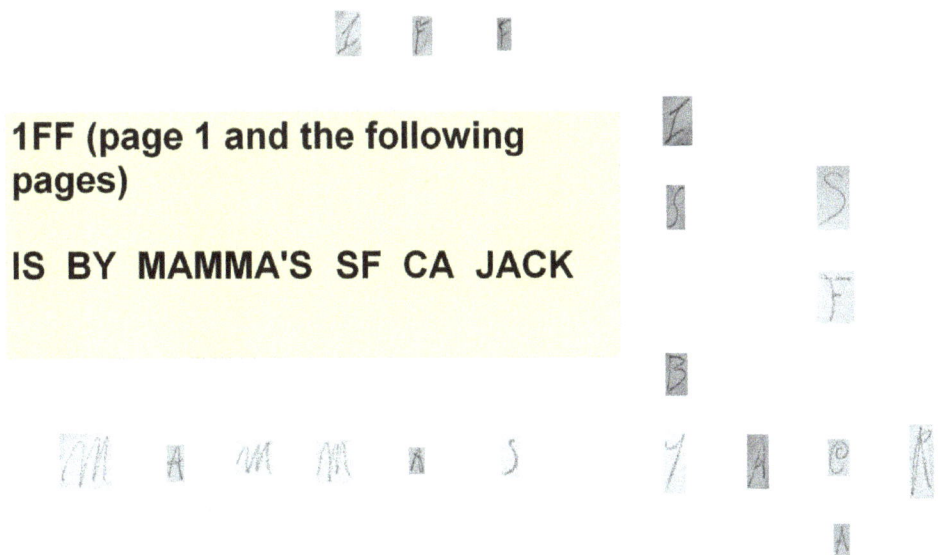

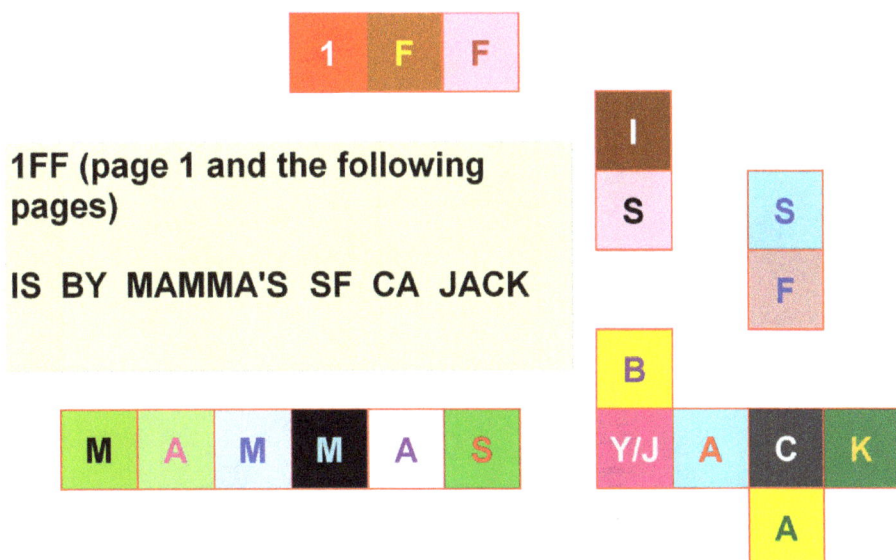

1FF (page 1 and the following pages)

IS BY MAMMA'S SF CA JACK

1FF (page 1 and the following pages)

IS BY MAMMA'S SF CA JACK

Here the word, "mamma", is an acceptable variant of "mama", and is therefore not misspelled. The abbreviation, "ff", is used in citation to refer to a section for which no final number can usefully be given (Wiktionary). The cursive capital, "J", is generated from the ambiguous, "Y". But before we accept the above as being a decrypted solution, let's go back to the other encrypted message to see if the first name "Jack" is correct.

1FF (page 1 and the following pages)

IS BY MAMMA'S SF CA JACK

S	F

	K
C	A

B	A
Y/J	

I
S

1FF (page 1 and the following pages)

IS BY MAMMA'S SF CA JACK

1	F	F

M	A	M	M	A	S

When we insert the first name of "Jack" into the previously unsolved encrypted note, here is the only reasonable solution that was generated:

LIPSTICK KILLER WALL CODE DECRYPTION - PAGE 4

"NINE BRIEF NOTES" SECTION

FEEL	NEAR	HOME	12
FOR	HE IS	ON TRACK	14
IF YOU	CAN	BELIEVE	15
MY 1ST	NAME	IS JACK	15

56

Skeptics may argue that the second line should read, "For you are on track", instead of, "For he is on track", and that hence, the above is an invalid force-fit solution. But, this is not the case. In the first line, the killer is implicitly and imperatively addressing "you". In the second line, the killer is figuratively turning his head and addressing the person sitting next to you to begrudgingly give you a compliment that you having gotten this far in your decryption efforts. In the third line, the killer has returned to addressing you directly. There is no significant "awkwardness" here that accompanies a force-fit solution. The solution above is reasonable and acceptable.

So let's now try to find the surname. We have one remaining encrypted note for the surname and then the last encrypted note that contains the whole name.

The following partially, potentially decrypted message is what we have so far with regards to generating a surname name for the killer. Here, as previously discussed, we are making a default assumption that the last name begins with the letter, "T", since that is the original letter from which the letter, "J", emerges. So, once again, now what do we do?

9

15

13

MY SURNAME IS T

19

56

Let's review what we know about this man named "Jack" so far:

- From the crossword puzzle solution, Jack is somehow associated with SF, CA; which we can safely assume to be San Francisco, California.

- We can hypothesize that Jack either was born in San Francisco, or lives in San Francisco, or works in San Francisco, or grew up in San Francisco.
- There is the possibility that Jack does not live in Chicago.
- It is probable that Jack is a citizen of the United States of America.
- From the "capital letters" crossword puzzle solution, we can deduce that he may have an inordinate affection for his mother.
- At the time of the murder, it is probable that his mother is still living.
- Jack is probably not an elderly man, for example, probably not someone in his sixties or seventies.
- Jack is a physically capable person who is extremely intelligent.
- As previously mentioned, Jack's native tongue is probably American English.
- Josephine Ross was probably not the first person Jack had ever killed.
- As mentioned before, Jack's last name is going to probably be not too difficult to spell or pronounce in American English, including the possibility that his surname has been anglicized.
- Since in English, the name "Jack" is traditionally used as the diminutive form of the given name John, it is possible that our "Jack" here may also possibly be named "John".
- Jack may possibly have a background related to code encryption and decryption, that is, code breaking.
- Jack probably has a history of mental instability and has exhibited anti-social behavior on more than one occasion.
- Jack's childhood may have been far from the norm.
- Jack is probably not associated with any religious organization and is probably not a religious person.

Here historical eyewitness accounts of possible murderers in the Ross and Brown case are not being included since they are somewhat vague and appear to differ widely and hence, are not considered here to be reliable.

So why is Jack in Chicago? Does he live there or is he on business there? Or is he just on vacation or visiting someone?

So an interesting hypothetical question is, if the early Chicago investigators had the information above on the killer named "Jack", and assuming that they would have launched a nationwide search for a man matching the above description, could they have made an arrest without having the killer's last name? The odds are probably not.

Based on unpublished work by the author of this book, the name of Jack (aka John) Tarrance was generated from the decryption of messages associated with various murders. In one of these decrypted messages, Jack states, "Hint John a lad home thrice cut windy city females!" It was this decrypted message that led the author of this book to investigate the potential connection between the Lipstick Murders and John (Jack) Tarrance. Hence, here is what the decrypted note now looks like:

LIPSTICK KILLER WALL CODE DECRYPTION - PAGE 5

"NINE BRIEF NOTES" SECTION

| V E I L | I S | O F F | 9 |

| I | F E E L | A B H O R R E N C E | 15 |

| C O M E | L E A R N | T H A T | 13 |

| M Y | S U R N A M E | I S | T A R R A N C E | 19 |

56

The surname "Tarrance" is pronounced like "Torrance", not, "Tearrance".

"NINE BRIEF NOTES" SECTION

9 15 13 19 56

VEIL
IS
OFF
ABHORRENCE
THAT
IS
I
FEEL
LEARN
SURNAME
COME
MY
TARRANCE

So, now that we have the killer's surname, we can decrypt the last encrypted message.

LAST NOTE OF NINE — 14

SO HERE ILL BE — 11

JACK TARRANCES HOME — 17

FEAR EVIL FROM ME — 14

56

So, according to this, the killer claims his home is in Chicago. Earlier we saw that the 19 capital letters crossword puzzle solution suggested that the killer Jack was either born in San Francisco, or lives in San Francisco, or works in San Francisco, or grew up in San Francisco. Do we have a possible contradiction of decrypted solutions here? Before we answer this, let's take a look at another tool in our decryption toolbox. This time, let's look at the group of 37 small letters only and form a cross-word puzzle like we did with the capital letters. When we do this, the only reasonable solution that was found is as follows:

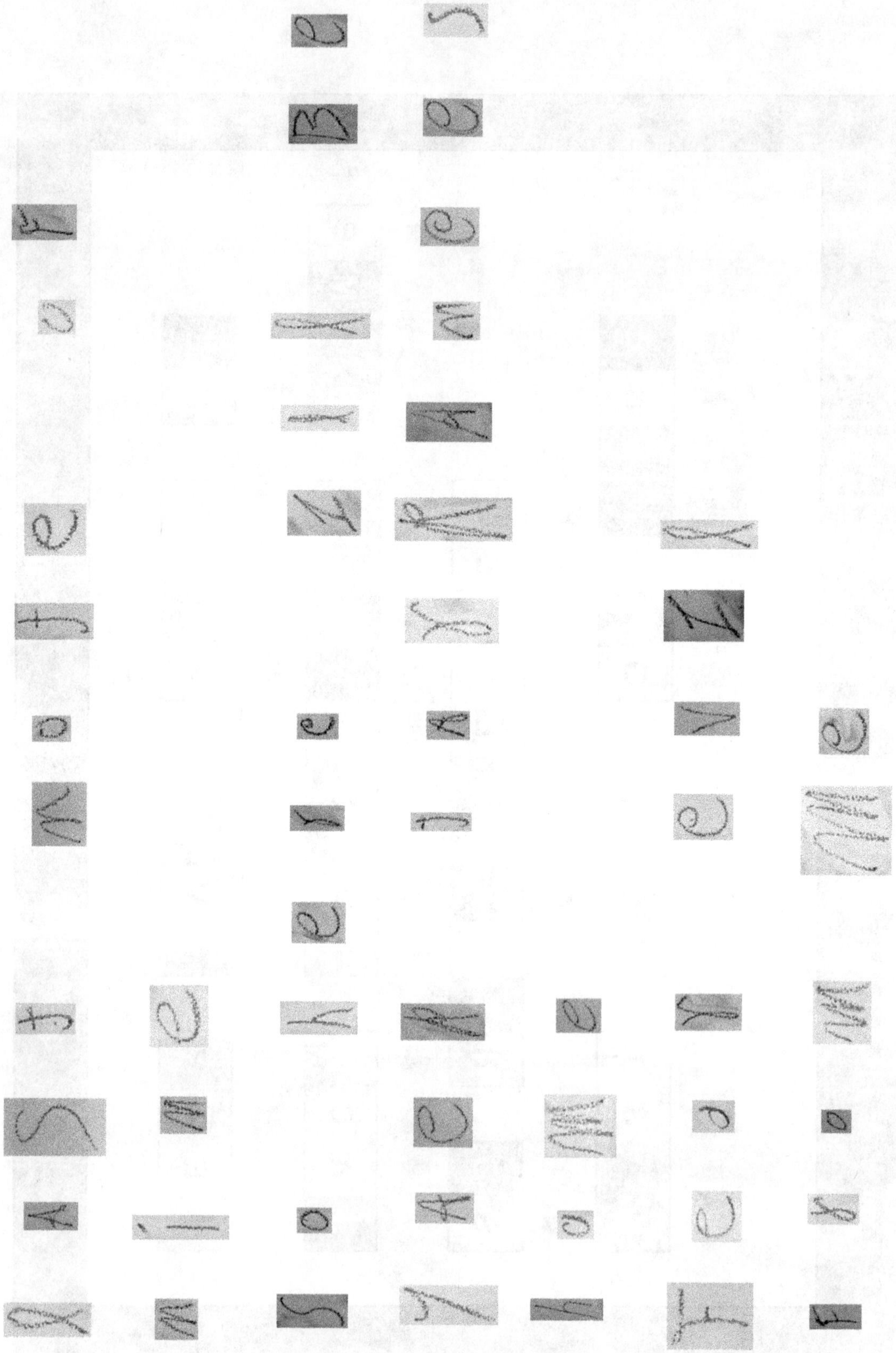

LIPSTICK
KILLER WALL
CODE
DECRYPTION -

SMALL
LETTERS ONLY

NINE

MORE HERE...

THE CLEVER
JACK
TARRANCE
KILLER

N	I	N	E

LIPSTICK
KILLER WALL
CODE
DECRYPTION -

SMALL
LETTERS ONLY

		H
M	O	R	E
		E

| . | . | . |

NINE

MORE HERE...

THE CLEVER
JACK
TARRANCE
KILLER

		T	
	J	A	C	K
T		R		I
H		R		L
E/C	L	E	V	E	R	L
		A		E
		N		R
		C
		E

NINE

MORE HERE...

THE CLEVER
JACK
TARRANCE
KILLER

| N | I | N | E |

LIPSTICK KILLER
WALL CODE
DECRYPTION -
SMALL
LETTERS ONLY

H	E	R	E

| M | O | R | E |

J	A	C	K

| T | A | R | R | A | N | C | E |

| T | H | E | L | E | V | E |

E / C

This "small-letter-only" decrypted solution importantly confirms the name of "Jack Tarrance" (this time spelled without the use of the ambiguous letter "Y" as a "J") as the killer, and even shows him bragging and taunting about being a "clever" killer.

The three small letter "o"s now form an ellipsis, which is the first time this ambiguous use of these three small letter "o"s has been "activated".

The appearance of the word "nine" confirms that Note 1's message of "nine brief notes" is decrypted correctly. The word "nine" indicates that this decrypted message is the continuation part of note nine and that the "more here…." signifies that there is more here to be decrypted and that there are possibly even more notes than the previous nine notes to be decrypted. So, do more notes than the "nine brief notes" exist? Upon further investigation, and in response to the questions raised by the decryption of note number nine, the following decryption was generated:

LIPSTICK KILLER WALL CODE DECRYPTION - PAGE 11

SECTION WHERE SOME OFF-RHYMES CAN OCCUR

REALLY MAKE RES — 14

IN CALIFORNIA — 11

BEEN HERE OFTEN — 17

TO SEE MOTHER MS FLOVA — 14

56

SECTION WHERE SOME OFF-RHYMES CAN OCCUR

REALLY 14

MAKE RES 11

IN CALIFORNIA 17

BEEN HERE OFTEN MS 14

TO SEE MOTHER FLOVA 56

Information reconciliation from various internet sources of uncertain reliability indicates that, "Flova", is the name of the killer's mother. This reference to "Flova", Jack Tarrance's mother, is consistent with the earlier decrypted phrase, "MAMMA'S SF CA JACK", which was generated from the 19 capital letters crossword puzzle solution.

The generated decrypted phrase that he "had been here [Chicago] often" is again consistent with the decrypted message from the 19 capital letters crossword puzzle solution that the killer probably had an inordinate affection for his mother.

The generation of the new relatively long word, "California", is a confirmation of the 19 capital letters crossword puzzle solution that suggested that the killer Jack could have lived in San Francisco. So, it is probable that the killer, Jack Tarrance, was in Chicago temporarily to visit his mother. And since Jack was probably not born or raised in San Francisco, California, he probably considered Chicago his "home", in a way, since that is where his mother lived. So the content of decrypted notes 9 and 11 really do not contradict each other.

Here skeptics might argue that the use of the word, "res", meaning "residence", is not properly spelled and therefore cannot be used as a part of a valid decrypted solution. But, when one considers this word as a slang word, then the slang word, "res", is actually spelled correctly and its use also fits in perfectly with the message.

Note here that the preceding decrypted note does not actually "rhyme", but "off-rhymes". Isn't this breaking the "rules" that were earlier established by the killer for the nine brief notes and wouldn't this make the above decrypted solution an invalid force-fit? Not really, because the old rules are now being displaced with new rules, which are different for a new "second layer" of encrypted notes. The "nine brief notes" that were just decrypted, which are just the first layer of decrypted notes, are only a subset of a larger set of encrypted notes, as explained by the following instructions from the new first note decryption:

SECTION WHERE SOME OFF-RHYMES CAN OCCUR

1	1
AS THERE ARE FOURTEEN	18
NOTES COMBINED	13
ILL MAKE SEVERAL	14
IN OFF RHYME	10
	56

Note the decrypted note above also "off-rhymes" like the earlier decrypted note 11.

The number "1" resets the counting of the decrypted notes. The word, "several", means more than two but not many.

So now we have three more notes to decrypt, and at least one of them must be a note that off-rhymes.

As mentioned earlier, the "nine brief notes" that were just decrypted are now a subset of these new fourteen notes. So, let's look at the next decrypted note:

LIPSTICK KILLER WALL CODE DECRYPTION - PAGE 1

SECTION WHERE SOME OFF-RHYMES CAN OCCUR

1

18

13

14

10

56

1

AS

THERE ARE FOURTEEN

NOTES COMBINED

MAKE SEVERAL

ILL

OFF RHYME

IN

SECTION WHERE SOME OFF-RHYMES CAN OCCUR

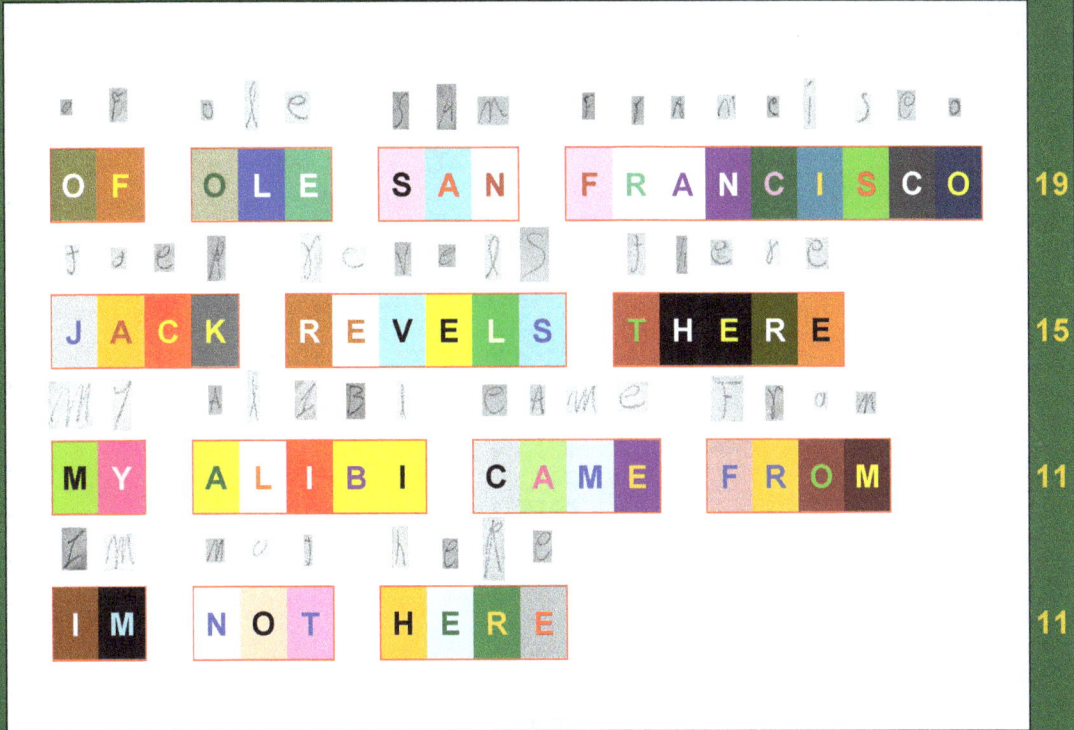

O F	O L E	S A N	F R A N C I S C O	19
J A C K	R E V E L S	T H E R E		15
M Y	A L I B I	C A M E	F R O M	11
I M	N O T	H E R E		11
				56

Here we have our third "off-rhyme" decrypted note.

Here for the first time, the name of "San Francisco" is spelled out and is not abbreviated. The generation of the word, "San Francisco", is consistent with the 19 capital letters crossword puzzle solution that suggested that the killer Jack could have lived in San Francisco. The generation of this word "San Francisco" is also consistent with the word, "California", which was earlier generated in decrypted note number 11.

Note here that the word, "revels", is consistent with the personality profile of Jack Tarrance that has been generated so far, and that it implies that he is not an elderly man, but probably a younger man who likes to have a "good time".

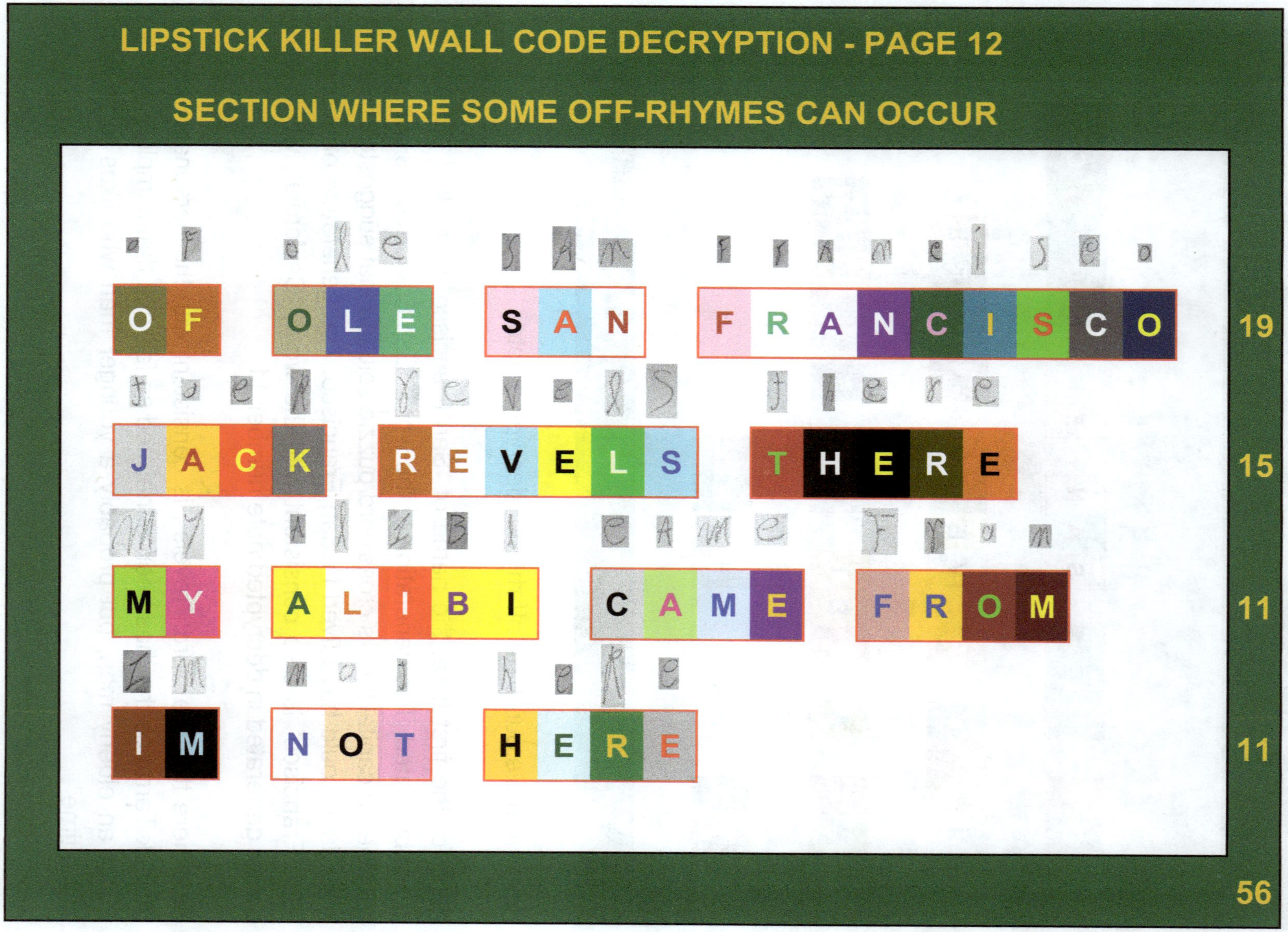
LIPSTICK KILLER WALL CODE DECRYPTION - PAGE 12
SECTION WHERE SOME OFF-RHYMES CAN OCCUR
OF OLE SAN FRANCISCO 19
JACK REVELS THERE 15
MY ALIBI CAME FROM 11
IM NOT HERE 11
56

To better understand the significance of the word, "alibi", let's look at the next decrypted note, which once again is derived from information reconciliation from various internet sources:

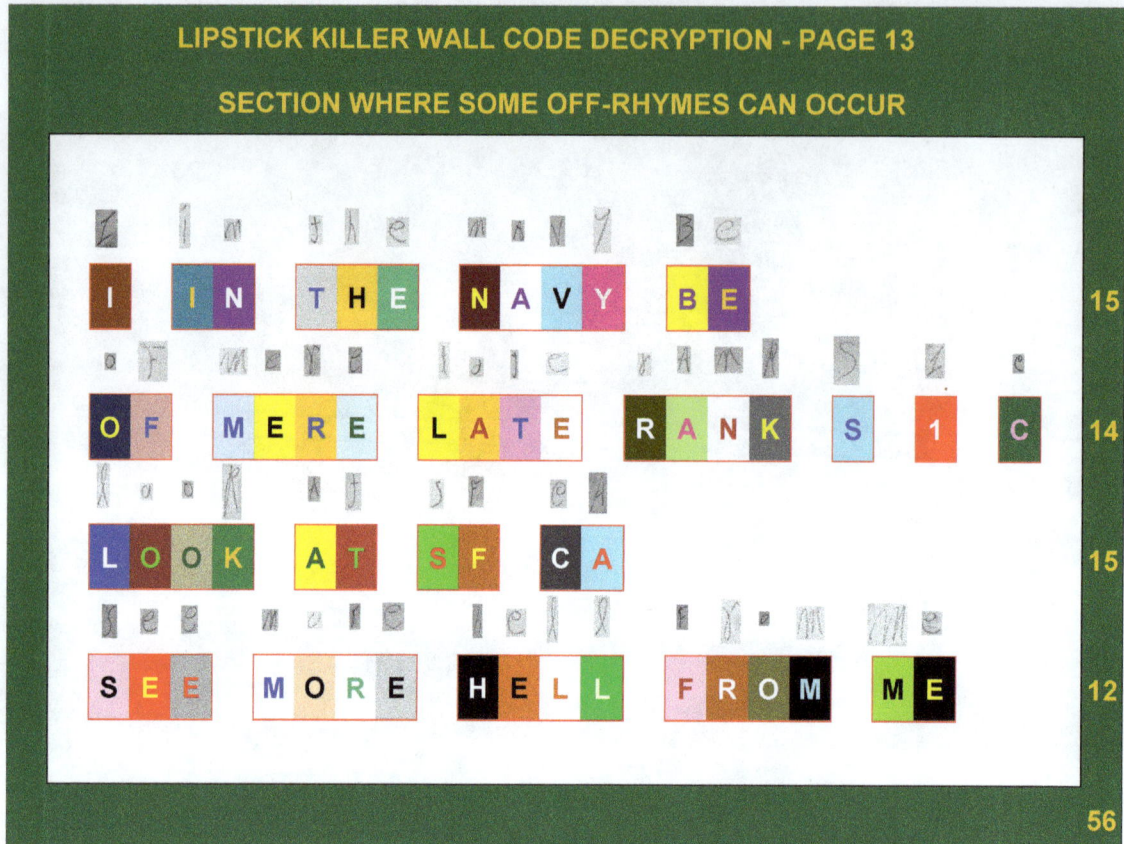

LIPSTICK KILLER WALL CODE DECRYPTION - PAGE 13

SECTION WHERE SOME OFF-RHYMES CAN OCCUR

I IN THE NAVY BE — 15

OF MERE LATE RANKS S 1 C — 14

LOOK AT SF CA — 15

SEE MORE HELL FROM ME — 12

56

So, apparently Jack is a young man serving in the Navy in the San Francisco, California area. His naval rank is Seaman First Class" (S1c).

It appears that if Jack goes through proper channels and gets an *authorized* leave to go visit his mother in Chicago, then he does not and cannot really have an alibi, since it would be documented that he was indeed in Chicago during the time of the murder. Hence, his visit to Chicago to see his mother Flova was probably an *unauthorized* visit and hence, not documented in his naval records. In the unlikely case Chicago investigators came to question Jack as a suspect, he would probably have had an airtight alibi.

SECTION WHERE SOME OFF-RHYMES CAN OCCUR

15

14

15

12

56

I IN THE NAVY BE

OF MERE LATE RANK S 1 C

LOOK AT SF CA

SEE MORE HELL FROM ME

Also note here that this decryption rhymes. It does not have to be an "off-rhyme" as we have already met the requirements of having generated "several" off-rhymes for this second layer of decrypted notes.

Here the abbreviation of "SF, CA" again confirms the location of San Francisco, California previously referred to in other decrypted notes.

The expression, "see more hell from me", does not necessarily mean that he is going on a murder spree in the same area that he lives in. It is probably used here more as a general expression meaning to "watch out" for him in order to frighten the readers of this decrypted message.

So, let's now look at the final decrypted message of the second layer of notes:

LIPSTICK KILLER WALL CODE DECRYPTION - PAGE 14

SECTION WHERE SOME OFF-RHYMES CAN OCCUR

IN CONCLUSION   12

CONTROVERSY   11

IF HERE A FALSE TALE   16

IF THERE MADE BY MR ME   17

56

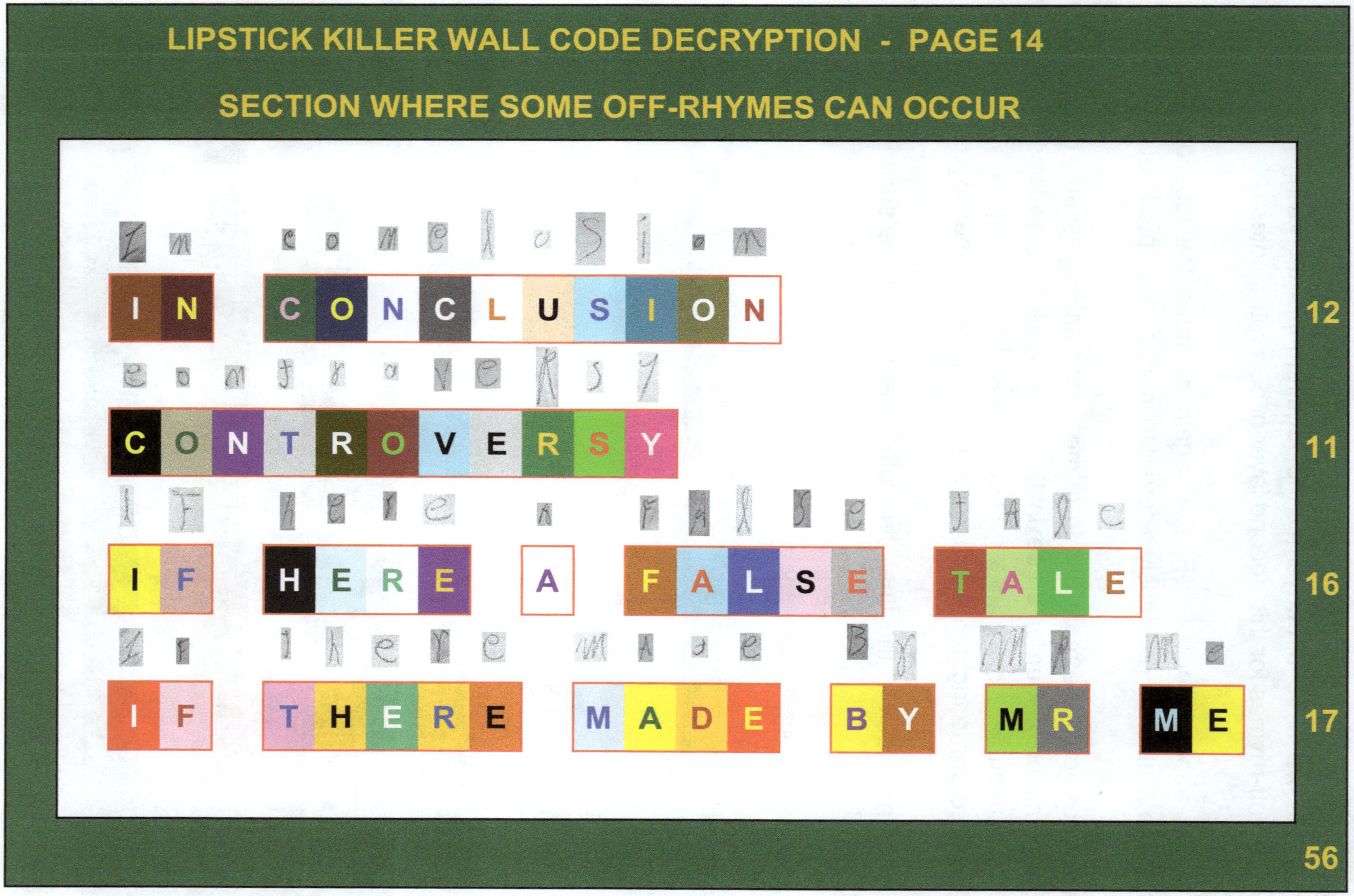
LIPSTICK KILLER WALL CODE DECRYPTION - PAGE 14
SECTION WHERE SOME OFF-RHYMES CAN OCCUR
IN CONCLUSION 12
CONTROVERSY 11
IF HERE A FALSE TALE 16
IF THERE MADE BY MR ME 17
56

The killer is now attempting to "play with the minds" of the readers of the note. However, the fact that this message fits in perfectly with the other messages, supports the facts that, yes, this "tale" is not false.

So, two layers of notes have now been decrypted and that should wrap it up, right? After all, the note above states, "In conclusion…", so, that confirms we are finished, right? No, we are not finished. Let's look at another decrypted message **from the group of small letters only:**

CLUE
HERE OVER
THE END HERE
NOTE NINETEEN
DONE

JACK
KILLER

LIPSTICK KILLER WALL CODE DECRYPTION - SMALL LETTERS ONLY

CLUE
HERE OVER
THE END HERE
NOTE NINETEEN
DONE

JACK
KILLER

LIPSTICK KILLER WALL CODE DECRYPTION - SMALL LETTERS ONLY

CLUE
HERE OVER
THE END HERE
NOTE NINETEEN
DONE

JACK KILLER

The preceding small letter only decrypted message is meant to be the second part of a future and final note nineteen, which will be the last note. But thus far, we have only fourteen decrypted notes, hence, we need to generate five more notes in order to make a total of nineteen notes.

What is needed then, is at least a third layer of notes, as the next decrypted message implies below. However, it only goes up to seventeen notes instead of the eventually needed nineteen notes:

LIPSTICK KILLER WALL CODE DECRYPTION - PAGE 1

SECTION WHERE NOTES DO NOT RHYME

1

I DO AFFIRM — 9

ALL SEVENTEEN BRIEF — 17

NOTES ON HERE ARE REAL — 18

SOME TO RHYME — 11

56

We now have a third layer of notes, which contains a total of seventeen notes. And since (including the new note 1 above) we now have a total of fifteen notes, we then need two more notes to make a total of seventeen notes. These new two new notes will not rhyme inside the note. However,

SECTION WHERE NOTES DO NOT RHYME

1 9 17 18 11 56

1

I DO

AFFIRM

SEVENTEEN

BRIEF

REAL

ARE

HERE

ON

RHYME

TO

ALL

NOTES

SOME

they can and will rhyme with each other, as the two new following decrypted notes depict:

SECTION WHERE NOTES DO NOT RHYME

THE REASON BECAUSE   16

I KILL HER IS FOR   13

MERE EVIL ENJOYMENT   17

AND FOR FAME   10

56

SECTION WHERE NOTES DO NOT RHYME

REMEMBER   8

AS I DO NOT FEEL   12

SORRY FOR THE VICTIM   17

I CAN FEEL NO REAL SHAME   19

56

SECTION WHERE NOTES DO NOT RHYME

THE REASON I KILL

BECAUSE IS HER

IS FOR ENJOYMENT EVIL

FOR FAME

MERE AND

16

13

17

10

56

LIPSTICK KILLER WALL CODE DECRYPTION - PAGE 17

SECTION WHERE NOTES DO NOT RHYME

REMEMBER 8

AS I DO NOT FEEL 12

SORRY FOR THE VICTIM 17

I CAN FEEL NO REAL SHAME 19

56

The fact that these two notes rhyme with each indicates that it follows the sequence of:

1) The first layer of nine notes rhyming with each other
2) The second layer of notes being able to off-rhyme
3) This third layer of notes not rhyming with itself but rhyming with each other
4) The last two notes, which make the fourth and final layer of notes, not rhyming with itself or rhyming with each other

The previous last two notes are interesting in that the killer finally answers the "Why?" question and conveys his reasons for killing his victims.

The next new note 1 of the fourth and final layer of notes read as follows:

1

| 1 | | | | | | | | | | | | 1 |

HI MR FOOL ... 8

FIRM FACTS ARE ... 12

NINETEEN NOTES OVERALL ... 20

ARE USED HERE BY ME ... 15

56

1   8   12   20   15   56

1

HI

MR

FIRM

FOOL

FACTS

ARE

NINETEEN

NOTES

OVERALL

HERE

ARE

USED

BY

ME

So now we need only one more note to complete the fourth layer of notes and to also complete the entire set of 19 notes. What follows is the second note of the fourth layer and the final and concluding note:

The contents of this note are somewhat ironic in that the original lipstick wall message stated, "For heavens [sic] sake catch me…" while in this final nineteenth note the killer taunts that you can "never catch me". And sadly, the killer was correct, he was never caught.

The overall layout of the decrypted messages, that is, the arrangement and connectivity of the four layers of notes and crossword messages, are depicted in the appendices.

LIPSTICK KILLER WALL CODE DECRYPTION - PAGE 19

LAST SECTION

LEARN	5
YOU CAN NEVER CATCH ME	18
FOR I AM SMARTER	13
FEEL SLIER	9
JOB FINISHED	11
	56

CONCLUDING REMARKS / MISCELLANEOUS COMMENTS

- No more encrypted messages were detected in the cursive-letters-only group or the printed-letters-only group (see appendices for their listings). Mathematically speaking, this makes sense in that the degrees of freedom left for the originator of the encrypted messages had "run out". That is, there was nothing left over in the cursive-letters-only group or the printed-letters-only group "to work with" in order to generate more meaningful encrypted messages.

- All listed ambiguous characters and all capital letters have been "activated" in the decrypted messages. That is, all values of the listed ambiguous characters and all capital letters were used at least once in the provided decrypted messages.

- Due to the complex nature of decrypting the Lipstick Killer wall message, the author of this book did not reveal all the decryption techniques that were used to provide decryption solutions.

- The reader should be advised here that the amount of *incorrect* information that can be found on the internet concerning Jack Tarrance is enormous.

- Ironically, despite the ungodly nature of this crime, no foul language was used by the killer in his decrypted messages. If the killer had used foul language, the killer knew that the eventually decrypted messages would not be revealed to the public, which would deprive the killer of his "glory".

- The possibility exists that both Josephine Ross and Frances Brown were selected and killed in part due to the fact that their names were compatible with the almost finished, soon-to-be encrypted wall message that was written in Lipstick.

- Josephine Ross and Frances Brown were also selected in part because the killer had absolutely no relationship of any type with these individuals. Hence, as a part of a perfect crime, the killer, having no connection to these individuals, could not be traced. The selection of Josephine Ross and Frances Brown was also to impress upon the public these were essentially typical, average citizens who were selected at random by the killer, which implies no real motive by the killer for having selected these particular individuals. This strategy was designed to terrorize the public, knowing that they or their loved ones could be the next victim.

- From an encryption point of view, the first name "Frances" is compatible with the encryption required word, "San Francisco".

- It should be noted that very few words rhyme with the surname "Tarrance" (pronounced as "Torrance"). About the only word that can be easily used in a decrypted message is the word, "abhorrence". Hence, this is what could have been the true encryption requirements for the letter "B" instead of the surname, "Brown".

- There is a high probability that the killer brought a written copy of the wall message with him to Miss Brown's apartment. It was probably written on paper, folded and placed into one of his pockets.

- The killer was not too young to have devised such a murder or to have written such an encrypted message.

- It is possible that the Lipstick killer chose relatively simple encryption techniques (anagram segments, crosswords, etc.) in order to intellectually humiliate his perceived adversaries. Part of the motivation for creating this wall message was to embarrass and humiliate officials associated with law enforcement, that is, the killer wanted them to know that they were no match for his cunning nature and his superior intelligence.

- It was initially the killer's goal to have these decrypted messages eventually revealed to the public in order to get historical credit for what he considered to be brilliant work, that is, a historical criminal masterpiece. The killer did not want to be caught, but initially he eventually wanted to be known as the infamous genius who committed this perfect crime.

- The lipstick killer knew that, in the very unlikely event the wall message became decrypted, that the decrypted messages could never be successfully used in a court of law to convict him. He would walk free and yet be known as a criminal genius.

- In the author's opinion, it is probable, but not impossible, that the lone blurred impression from a finger joint found in Miss Brown's apartment did not belong to the killer.

- The Lipstick Killer was able to successfully mask his natural, normal handwriting. Any claims that this wall message, as a stand-alone piece of evidence, positively identifies the killer as Jack Tarrance, that is, positively matches samples of what are claimed to be Jack Tarrance's natural, normal handwriting, are invalid claims.

- Likewise, any claims that because Jack Tarrances's natural, normal handwriting (assuming such samples exist) does not match the wall message, therefore, Jack Tarrance could not have killed Miss Brown, are also invalid claims for the same basic reason – which is, Jack Tarrance was able to successfully disguise his natural, normal handwriting.

- Since there are only 56 characters that varied from about 2 to about 6 inches, and since the Lipstick killer pre-meditatively designed each painted or drawn (not handwritten) character to have an encrypted dimension, it is not exceedingly difficult nor impossible for the killer to have successfully disguised his handwriting for this particular case.

- In the following article, *HANDWRITING EXPERT DOUBTS MURDERER OF EX-WAVE SLEW CHILD,* Chicago Daily Tribune Jan 20, 1946; pg. 7; Rudolph B. Salmon, 30 N. La Salle St. of Chicago, Illinois; handwriting identification expert and attorney for more than 30 years, cast doubt on theories that the murderer of Frances Brown and the murderer of Suzanne Degnan are the same person. After an analysis of the message printed in lipstick on the wall of Frances Brown's room and the ransom note left In the Degnan child's room, he declared there were not sufficient, similar characterizations in the writings to justify an opinion that they were written by the same person.

- It is important to note here that Rudolph B. Salmon's analysis is correct, however, historical analysis will show that the murderer of Frances Brown and Suzanne Degnan were one and the same person. What this means is – that the killer of Frances Brown was successful in disguising his so-called handwriting from at least one handwriting expert.

- It is not uncommon in criminal cases, once all the forensic evidence has been already collected and the data overwhelmingly points to the guilt of a particular individual, for a so-called handwriting expert to then weigh in and then claim that they have positively identified the handwriting in question as belonging to the guilty party. And indeed they are correct, but only after the fact, and not due to true hand writing analysis.

- And yes, William Heirens, the man ultimately convicted for this crime, was innocent. The best recommended reading on this topic is the book, "*William Heirens His Day In Court*" by Dolores Kennedy.

APPENDIX

LIPSTICK KILLER WALL CODE DECRYPTION

THE DECRYPTED MESSAGES

Notes: (this page intentionally left blank)

LIPSTICK KILLER WALL CODE DECRYPTION - SUMMARY

LIPSTICK KILLER WALL CODE DECRYPTION
ORIGINAL WALL MESSAGE

FOR HEAVENS

SAKE CATCH ME

BEFORE I KILL MORE

I CANNOT CONTROL MYSELF

LIPSTICK KILLER WALL CODE DECRYPTION - PAGE 1
LAST SECTION

1

HI MR FOOL

FIRM FACTS ARE

NINETEEN NOTES OVERALL

ARE USED HERE BY ME

LIPSTICK KILLER WALL CODE DECRYPTION - PAGE 1
SECTION WHERE NOTES DO NOT RHYME

1

I DO AFFIRM

ALL SEVENTEEN BRIEF

NOTES ON HERE ARE REAL

SOME TO RHYME

LIPSTICK KILLER WALL CODE DECRYPTION - PAGE 1
SECTION WHERE SOME OFF-RHYMES CAN OCCUR

1

AS THERE ARE FOURTEEN

NOTES COMBINED

I'LL MAKE SEVERAL

IN OFF RHYME

LIPSTICK KILLER WALL CODE DECRYPTION - PAGE 1
NINE BRIEF NOTES SECTION

NO 1

AS THERE ARE NINE BRIEF NOTES

FROM EVIL ME

READ THEM

SO CAREFULLY

LIPSTICK KILLER WALL CODE DECRYPTION - PAGE 2
NINE BRIEF NOTES SECTION

FOUR VERSES IN NOTE

MAKE FINAL LINE RHYME

EACH TO BEAR

TALES OF CRIME

LOOK OFF NOTES

FROM MY ADVICE

THE MAN A KILLER BE

SEE NAME RISE THRICE

FEEL NEAR HOME

FOR HE IS ON TRACK

IF YOU CAN BELIEVE

MY 1ST NAME IS JACK

VEIL IS OFF

I FEEL ABHORRENCE

COME LEARN THAT

MY SURNAME IS TARRANCE

HAVE JOSEFINE A ROSS

MY IL REFERENCE 1

BACK FROM HELL

I AM NOT YET DONE

LIPSTICK KILLER WALL CODE DECRYPTION - PAGE 7
NINE BRIEF NOTES SECTION

AT FRANCES BROUN

I CLEARLY SEE

KNIFE FROM NECK SHOT TO HEAD

I'M EVIL ME

LIPSTICK KILLER WALL CODE DECRYPTION - PAGE 8
NINE BRIEF NOTES SECTION

HEREOF I'LL MAKE

YES FEAR TO SEE

FROM A SMALL ONE

A VICTIM NUMBER THREE

LIPSTICK KILLER WALL CODE DECRYPTION - PAGE 9
NINE BRIEF NOTES SECTION

LAST NOTE OF NINE

SO HERE I'LL BE

JACK TARRANCE'S HOME

FEAR EVIL FROM ME

LIPSTICK KILLER WALL CODE DECRYPTION - PAGE 11
SECTION WHERE SOME OFF-RHYMES CAN OCCUR

REALLY MAKE RES

IN CALIFORNIA

BEEN HERE OFTEN

TO SEE MOTHER MS FLOVA

LIPSTICK KILLER WALL CODE DECRYPTION - PAGE 12
SECTION WHERE SOME OFF-RHYMES CAN OCCUR

OF OLE SAN FRANCISCO

JACK REVELS THERE

MY ALIBI CAME FROM

I'M NOT HERE

LIPSTICK KILLER WALL CODE DECRYPTION - PAGE 13
SECTION WHERE SOME OFF-RHYMES CAN OCCUR

I IN THE NAVY BE

OF MERE LATE RANK S 1 C

LOOK AT SF CA

SEE MORE HELL FROM ME

LIPSTICK KILLER WALL CODE DECRYPTION - PAGE 14
SECTION WHERE SOME OFF-RHYMES CAN OCCUR

IN CONCLUSION

CONTROVERSY

IF HERE A FALSE TALE

IF THERE MADE BY MR ME

LIPSTICK KILLER WALL CODE DECRYPTION - PAGE 16
SECTION WHERE NOTES DO NOT RHYME

THE REASON BECAUSE

I KILL HER IS FOR

MERE EVIL EMJOYMENT

AND FOR FAME

LIPSTICK KILLER WALL CODE DECRYPTION - PAGE 17
SECTION WHERE NOTES DO NOT RHYME

REMEMBER

AS I DO NOT FEEL

SORRY FOR THE VICTIM

I CAN FEEL NO REAL SHAME

LIPSTICK KILLER WALL CODE DECRYPTION - PAGE 19
LAST SECTION

LEARN

YOU CAN NEVER CATCH ME

FOR I AM SMARTER

FEEL SLIER

JOB FINISHED

APPENDIX

LIPSTICK KILLER WALL CODE DECRYPTION

PRINTED AND CURSIVE CHARACTERS

Notes: (this page intentionally left blank)

ENCIRCLED CHARACTERS INDICATE THE 23 PRINTED LETTERS ON THE WALL MESSAGE

LIPSTICK KILLER CODE DECRYPTION - PRINTED CHARACTERS

#	Character	Value
1	1/I	= TWO VALUES - "1" OR "I"
2	B	= ONE VALUE AS "B"
3	D/O/A	= THREE VALUES - "D" OR "O" OR "A"
4	F	= ONE VALUE AS "F"
5	F	= ONE VALUE AS "F"
6	F	= ONE VALUE AS "F"
7	H	= ONE VALUE AS "H"
8	H	= ONE VALUE AS "H"
9	I	= ONE VALUE AS "I"
10	I	= ONE VALUE AS "I"
11	J/T	= TWO VALUES - "J" OR "T"
12	J/T	= TWO VALUES - "J" OR "T"
13	J/T	= TWO VALUES - "J" OR "T"
14	O	= ONE VALUE AS "O"
15	O	= ONE VALUE AS "O"
16	O	= ONE VALUE AS "O"
17	O/A	= TWO VALUES - "O" OR "A"
18	S	= ONE VALUE AS "S"
19	S	= ONE VALUE AS "S"
20	S	= ONE VALUE AS "S"
21	U/O	= TWO VALUES - A "U" OR "O"
22	V	= ONE VALUE AS "V"
23	Y/J	= TWO VALUES - A "Y" OR "J"

LIPSTICK KILLER CODE DECRYPTION - CURSIVE CHARACTERS

#	Character	Color Code		Value
1		A	=	ONE VALUE AS "A"
2		A	=	ONE VALUE AS "A"
3		A	=	ONE VALUE AS "A"
4		A	=	ONE VALUE AS "A"
5		C/E	=	TWO VALUES - "C" OR "E"
6		C/E	=	TWO VALUES - "C" OR "E"
7		C/E	=	TWO VALUES - "C" OR "E"
8		C/E	=	TWO VALUES - "C" OR "E"
9		C/E	=	TWO VALUES - "C" OR "E"
10		C/E	=	TWO VALUES - "C" OR "E"
11		C/E	=	TWO VALUES - "C" OR "E"
12		C/E	=	TWO VALUES - "C" OR "E"
13		C/E	=	TWO VALUES - "C" OR "E"
14		C/E	=	TWO VALUES - "C" OR "E"
15		C/E	=	TWO VALUES - "C" OR "E"
16		C/E	=	TWO VALUES - "C" OR "E"
17		K/R	=	TWO VALUES - "K" OR "R"
18		K/R	=	TWO VALUES - "K" OR "R"
19		I/L	=	TWO VALUES - "I" OR "L"
20		L/I	=	TWO VALUES - "L" OR "I"
21		L/I	=	TWO VALUES - "L" OR "I"
22		L/I	=	TWO VALUES - "L" OR "I"

LIPSTICK KILLER CODE DECRYPTION - CURSIVE CHARACTERS

23		M	=	ONE VALUE AS "M"
24		M	=	ONE VALUE AS "M"
25		M	=	ONE VALUE AS "M"
26		N/M	=	TWO VALUES - "N" OR "M"
27		N/M	=	TWO VALUES - "N" OR "M"
28		N/M	=	TWO VALUES - "N" OR "M"
29		N/M	=	TWO VALUES - "N" OR "M"
30		R	=	ONE VALUE AS "R"
31		R	=	ONE VALUE AS "R"
32		R	=	ONE VALUE AS "R"
33		R/Y	=	TWO VALUES - "R" OR "Y"

APPENDIX

LIPSTICK KILLER WALL CODE DECRYPTION

OVERALL
LAYOUT OF DECRYPTED
MESSAGES

Notes: (this page intentionally left blank)

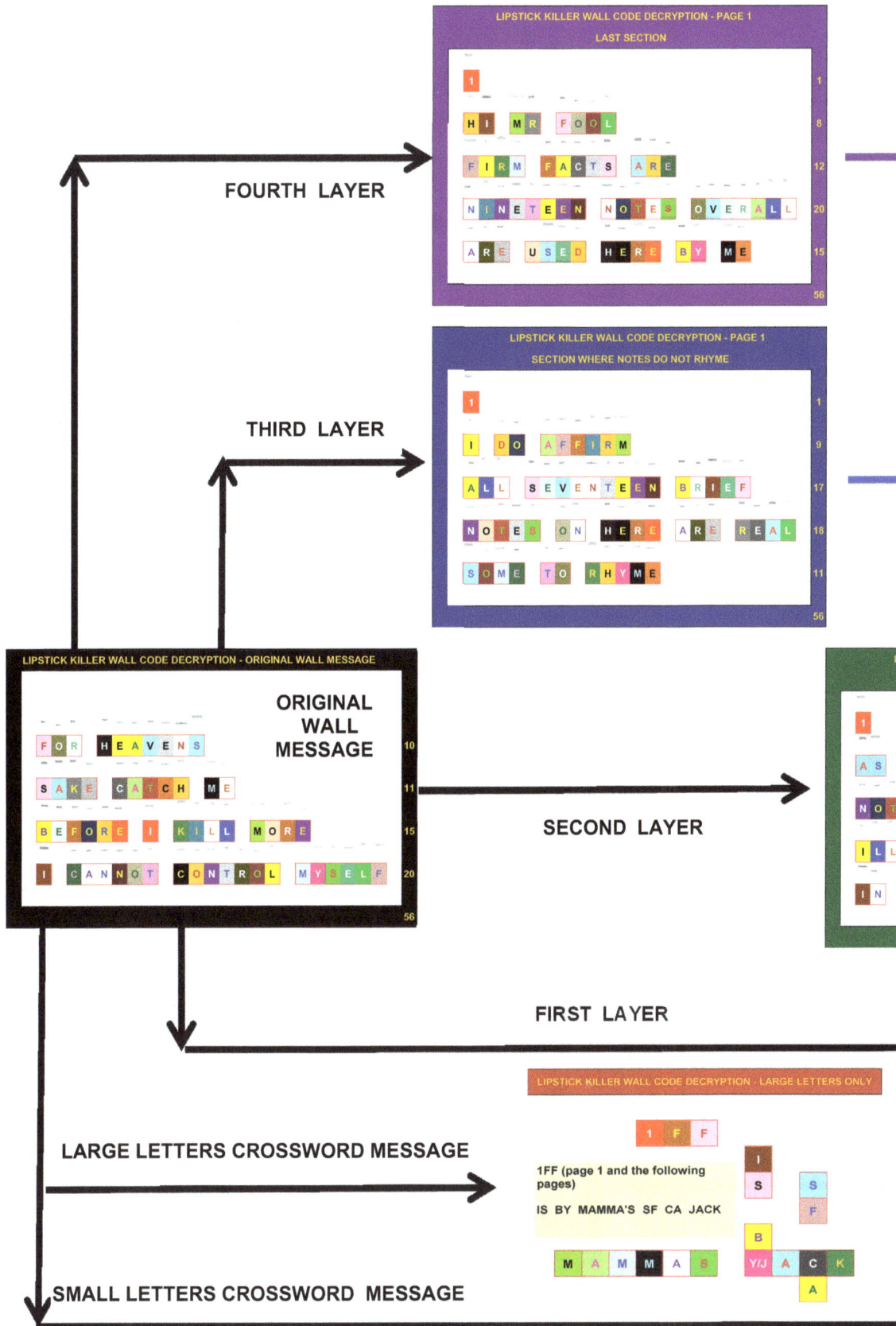

LIPSTICK KILLER WALL CODE DECRYPTION - PAGE 1
LAST SECTION

1

HI MR FOOL
FIRM FACTS ARE
NINETEEN NOTES OVERALL
ARE USED HERE BY ME

FOURTH LAYER

LIPSTICK KILLER WALL CODE DECRYPTION - PAGE 1
SECTION WHERE NOTES DO NOT RHYME

1

I DO AFFIRM
ALL SEVENTEEN BRIEF
NOTES ON HERE ARE REAL
SOME TO RHYME

THIRD LAYER

LIPSTICK KILLER WALL CODE DECRYPTION - ORIGINAL WALL MESSAGE

ORIGINAL
WALL
MESSAGE

FOR HEAVENS
SAKE CATCH ME
BEFORE I KILL MORE
I CANNOT CONTROL MYSELF

SECOND LAYER

1
AS
NOT
ILL
IN

FIRST LAYER

LIPSTICK KILLER WALL CODE DECRYPTION - LARGE LETTERS ONLY

1 F F

1FF (page 1 and the following pages)

IS BY MAMMA'S SF CA JACK

LARGE LETTERS CROSSWORD MESSAGE

I
S
S
F
B
M A M M A S   Y/J A C K
A

SMALL LETTERS CROSSWORD MESSAGE

R VERSES IN NOTE 16

E FINAL LINE RHYME 18

H TO BEAR 10

ES OF CRIME 12

56

LOOK OFF NOTES 12

FROM MY ADVICE 12

THE MAN A KILLER BE 15

SEE NAME RISE THRICE 17

56

FEEL NEAR HO

FOR HE IS ON

IF YOU CAN B

MY 1ST NAME

LIPSTICK KILLER WALL CODE DECRYPTION - PAGE 4
...S" SECTION

...ME   12

          ...TRACK   14

     ...ELIEVE   15

     ...IS JACK   15

                                               56

LIPSTICK KILLER WALL CODE DECRYPTION - PAGE 5
"NINE BRIEF NOTES" SECTION

VEIL IS OFF   9

I FEEL ABHORRENCE   15

COME LEARN THAT   13

MY SURNAME IS TARRANCE   19

                                               56

LIPSTICK KILLER WALL CODE DECRYPTION - PAGE 6
"NINE BRIEF NOTES" SECTION

HAVE JOSEFINE A ROSS

MY IL REFERENCE 1

BACK FROM HELL

I AM NOT YET DONE

LIPSTICK KILLER WALL CODE DECRYPTION - PAGE 7
"NINE BRIEF NOTES" SECTION

AT FRANCES BROUN   14
I CLEARLY SEE   11
KNIFE FROM NECK SHOT TO HEAD   23
IM EVIL ME   8
56

LIPSTICK KILLER WALL CODE DECRYPTION - PAGE 8
"NINE BRIEF NOTES" SECTION

HEREOF ILL MAKE
YES FEAR TO SEE
FROM A SMALL ONE
A VICTIM NUMBER THREE
56

LIPSTICK KILLER WALL CODE DECRYPTION - PAGE 11
SECTION WHERE SOME OFF-RHYMES CAN OCCUR

REALLY MAKE RES
IN CALIFORNIA
BEEN HERE OFTEN
TO SEE MOTHER MS FLOVA

14
11
17
14

56

LIPSTICK KILLE
SECTION WH

OF OL
JACK
MY AL
IM NO

LIPSTICK KILLER WALL CODE DECRYPTION - PAGE 9
"NINE BRIEF NOTES" SECTION

LAST NOTE OF NINE
SO HERE ILL BE
JACK TARRANCES HOME
FEAR EVIL FROM ME

13
12
13
18

14
11
17
14

56

56

LIPSTICK
KILLER WALL
CODE
DECRYPTION -

SMALL
LETTERS ONLY

NINE

MORE HERE...

THE CLEVER
JACK
TARRANCE

E SAN FRANCISCO	19
REVELS THERE	15
IBI CAME FROM	11
T HERE	11
	56

I IN THE NAVY BE	15
OF MERE LATE RANK S 1 C	14
LOOK AT SF CA	15
SEE MORE HELL FROM ME	12
	56

IN CONCLUSIO
CONTROVERSY
IF HERE A FA
IF THERE MAD

LIPSTICK KILLER WALL CODE DECRYPTION - PAGE 16
SECTION WHERE NOTES DO NOT RHYME

THE REASON BECAUSE 16
I KILL HER IS FOR 13
MERE EVIL ENJOYMENT 17
AND FOR FAME 10
56

LIPSTICK KILLER WALL CODE DECRYPTION - PAGE 17
SECTION WHERE NOTES DO NOT RHYME

REMEMBER
AS I DO NOT FEEL
SORRY FOR THE VICTIM
I CAN FEEL NO REAL SH

CRYPTION - PAGE 14
HYMES CAN OCCUR

N 12
11
LSE TALE 16
E BY MR ME 17
56

LIPSTICK KILLER WALL CODE DECRYPTION - PAGE 19

LAST SECTION

L E A R N   5

YOU CAN NEVER CATCH ME   18

FOR I AM SMARTER   13

FEEL SLIER   9

JOB FINISHED   11

56

A M E   19

8
12
17
19
56

LIPSTICK KILLER WALL CODE DECRYPTION - SMALL LETTERS ONLY

CLUE
HERE OVER
THE END HERE
NOTE NINETEEN
DONE

JACK
KILLER

Notes: (this page intentionally left blank)

APPENDIX

LIPSTICK   KILLER   WALL   CODE
DECRYPTION

LETTER

FREQUENCY

Notes: (this page intentionally left blank)

LIPSTICK KILLER WALL CODE LETTER FREQUENCY

		Count	Percent
1	A	4	7.1%
2	B	1	1.8%
3	C	3	5.4%
4	D	0	0.0%
5	E	9	16.1%
6	F	3	5.4%
7	G	0	0.0%
8	H	2	3.6%

		Count	Percent
9	I	3	5.4%
10	J	0	0.0%
11	K	2	3.6%
12	L	4	7.1%
13	M	3	5.4%
14	N	4	7.1%
15	O	6	10.7%
16	P	0	0.0%
17	Q	0	0.0%

		Count	Percent
18	R	4	7.1%
19	S	3	5.4%
20	T	3	5.4%
21	U	0	0.0%
22	V	1	1.8%
23	W	0	0.0%
24	X	0	0.0%
25	Y	1	1.8%
26	Z	0	0.0%

Totals	56	100.0%

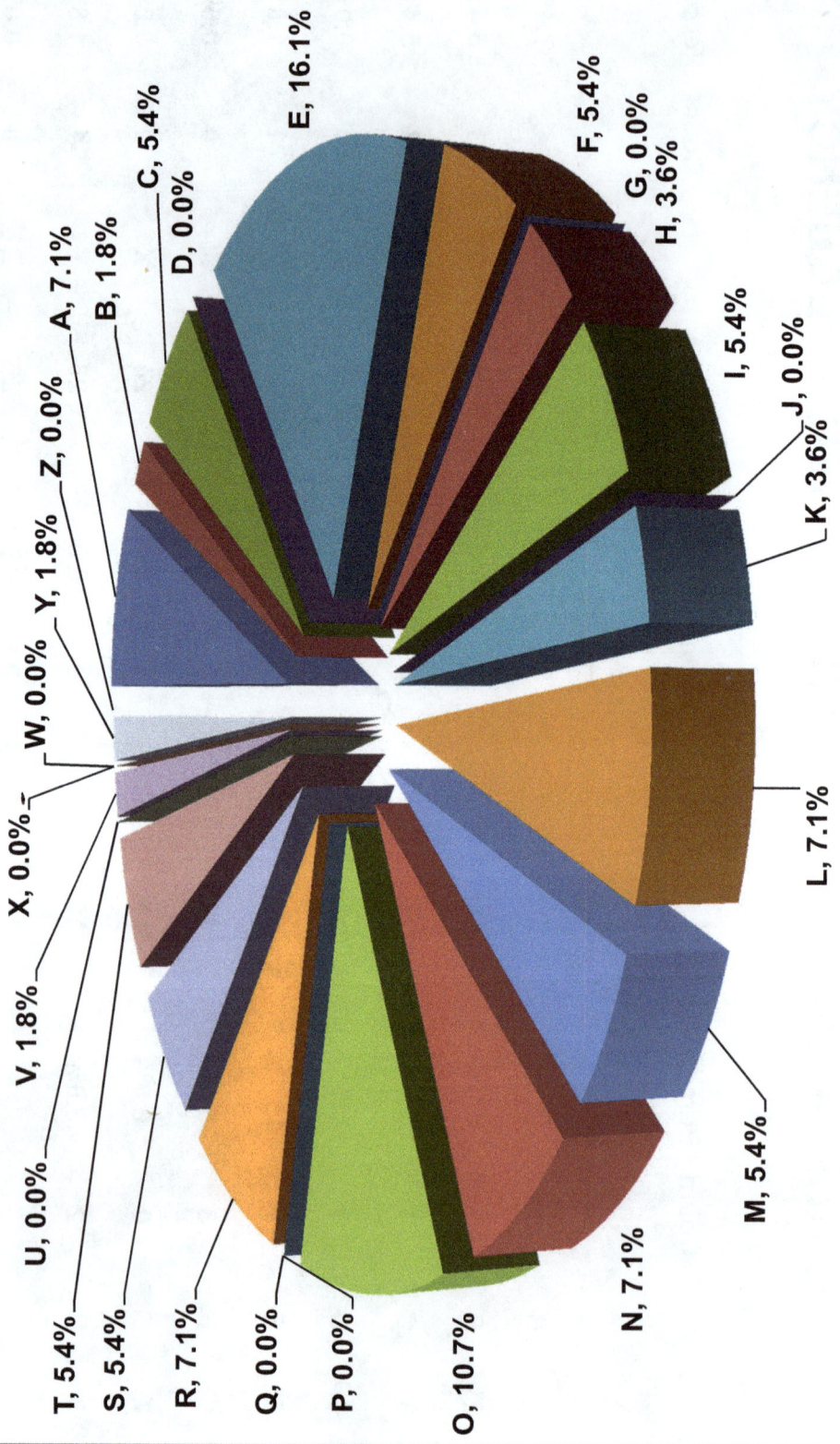

LIPSTICK KILLER WALL CODE LETTER FREQUENCY

A B C D E F G H I J K L M N O P Q R S T U V W X Y Z

A, 7.1%
B, 1.8%
C, 5.4%
D, 0.0%
E, 16.1%
F, 5.4%
G, 0.0%
H, 3.6%
I, 5.4%
J, 0.0%
K, 3.6%
L, 7.1%
M, 5.4%
N, 7.1%
O, 10.7%
P, 0.0%
Q, 0.0%
R, 7.1%
S, 5.4%
T, 5.4%
U, 0.0%
V, 1.8%
W, 0.0%
X, 0.0%
Y, 1.8%
Z, 0.0%

LIPSTICK KILLER WALL CODE LETTER FREQUENCY COMPARED TO NORMAL

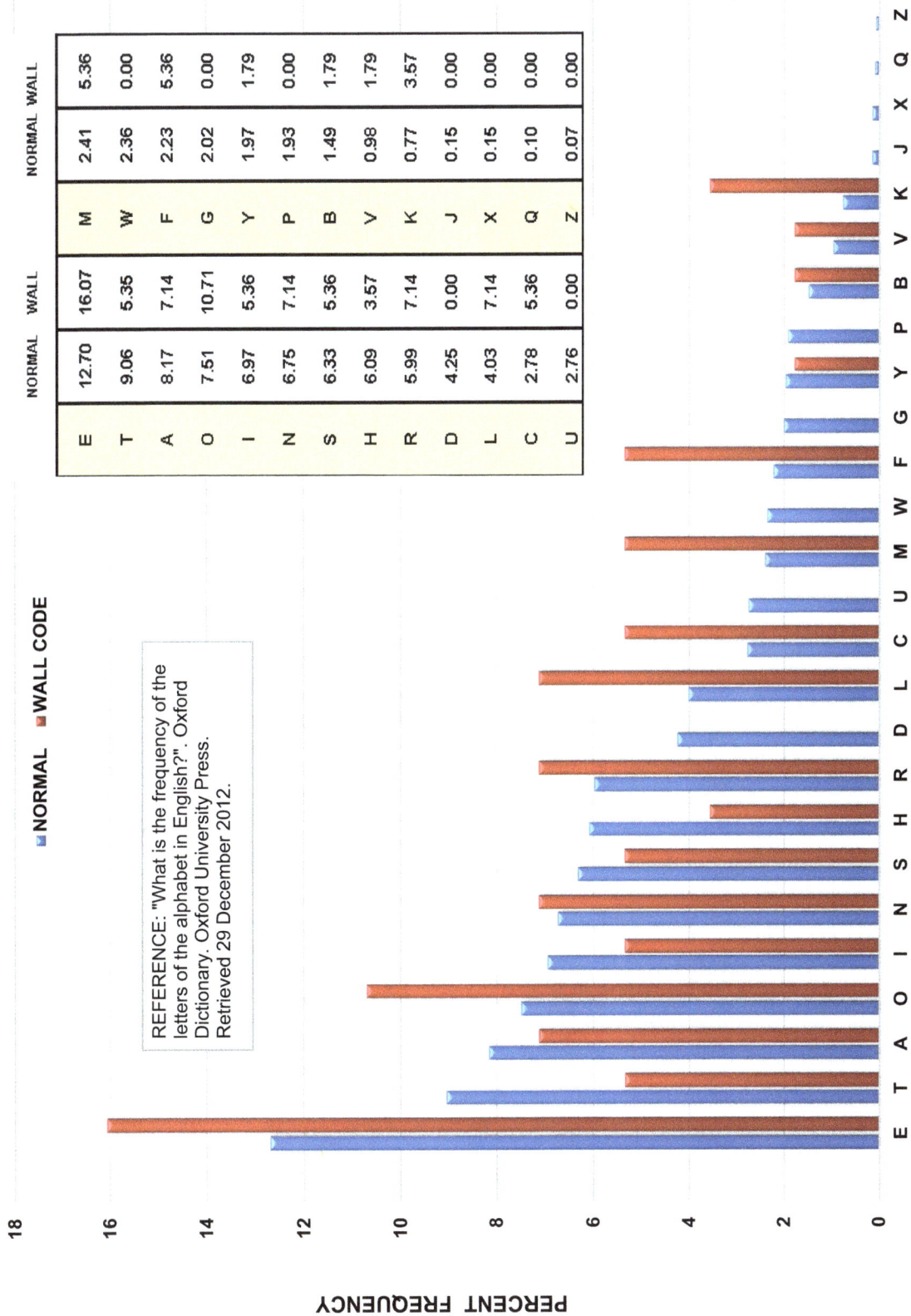

■ NORMAL ■ WALL CODE

	NORMAL	WALL		NORMAL	WALL
E	12.70	16.07	M	2.41	5.36
T	9.06	5.35	W	2.36	0.00
A	8.17	7.14	F	2.23	5.36
O	7.51	10.71	G	2.02	0.00
I	6.97	5.36	Y	1.97	1.79
N	6.75	7.14	P	1.93	0.00
S	6.33	5.36	B	1.49	1.79
H	6.09	3.57	V	0.98	1.79
R	5.99	7.14	K	0.77	3.57
D	4.25	0.00	J	0.15	0.00
L	4.03	7.14	X	0.15	0.00
C	2.78	5.36	Q	0.10	0.00
U	2.76	0.00	Z	0.07	0.00

REFERENCE: "What is the frequency of the letters of the alphabet in English?". Oxford Dictionary. Oxford University Press. Retrieved 29 December 2012.

PERCENT FREQUENCY

Notes: (this page intentionally left blank)

APPENDIX

LIPSTICK   KILLER   WALL   CODE DECRYPTION

ENLARGED CHARACTERS

Notes: (this page intentionally left blank)

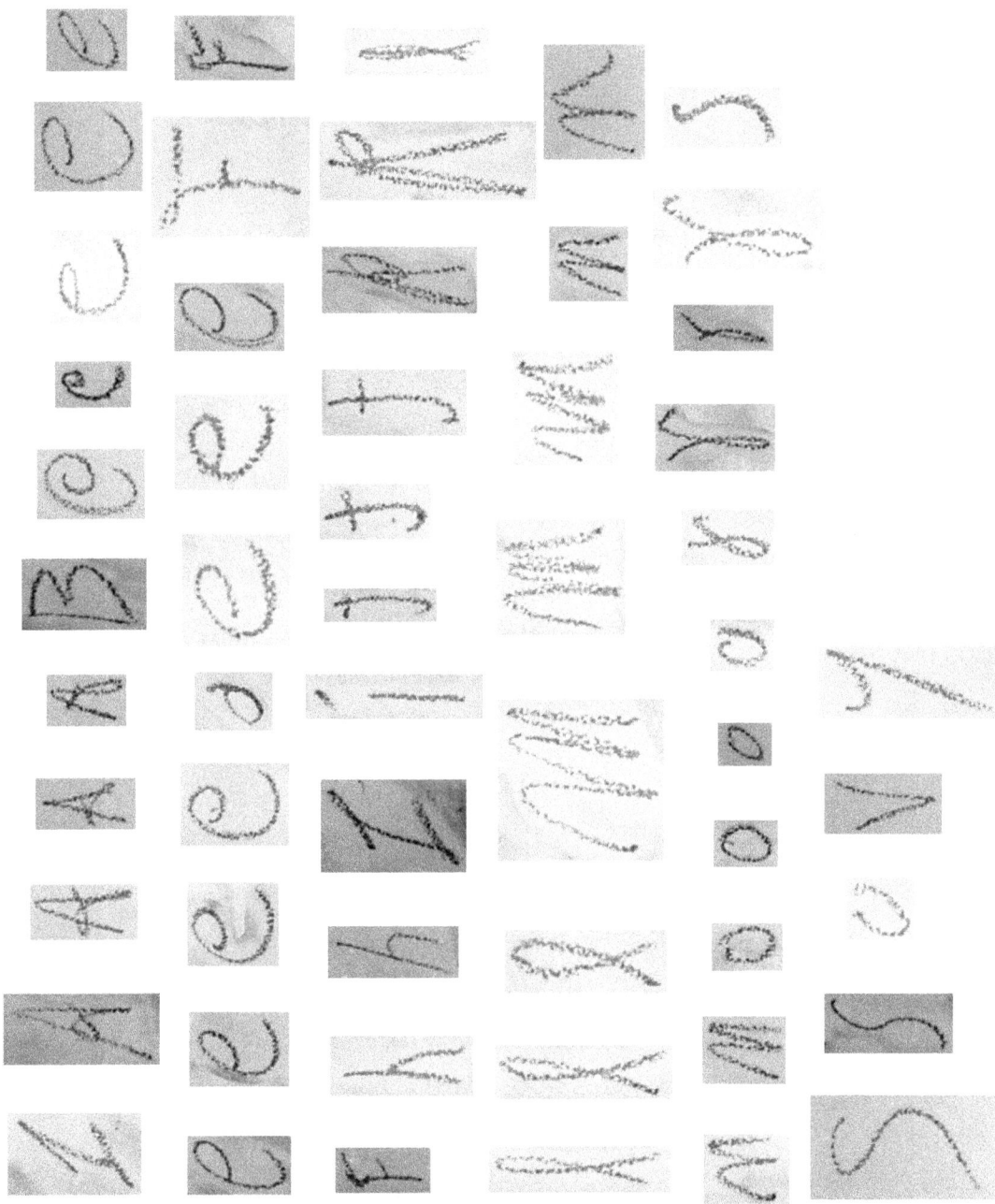

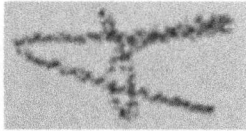
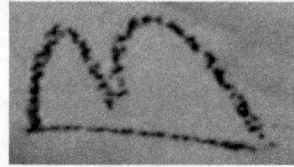
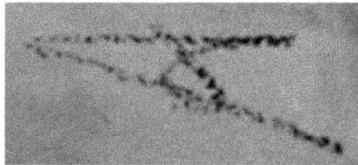

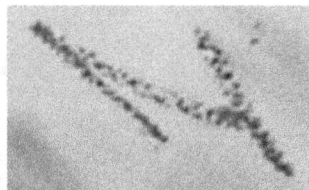

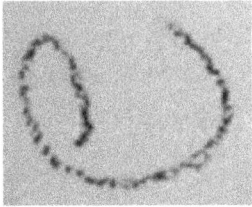

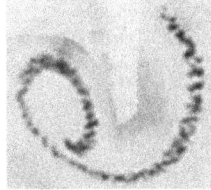

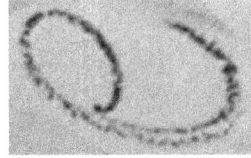

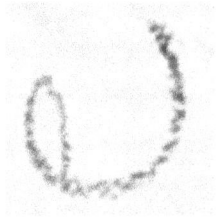

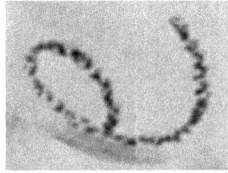

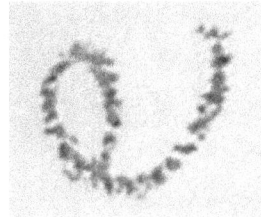

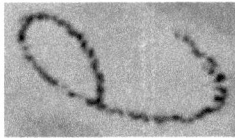

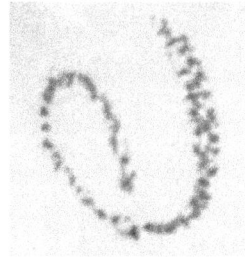

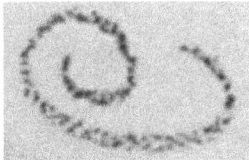

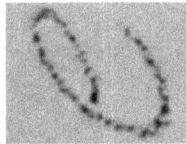

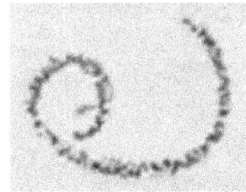

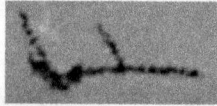

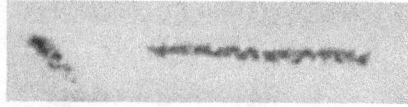

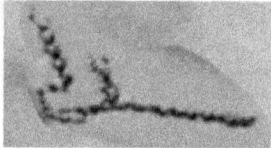

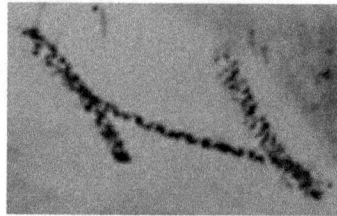

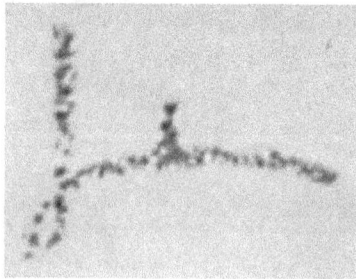

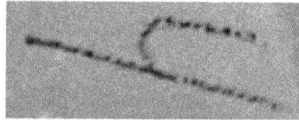

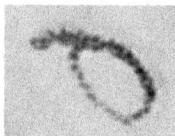

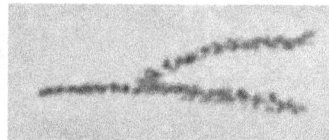

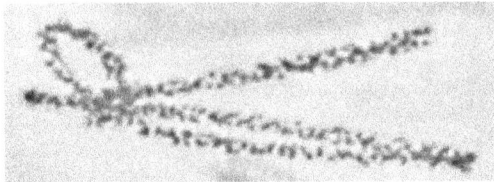

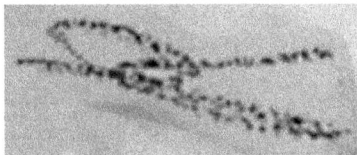

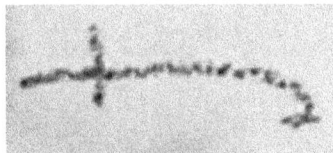

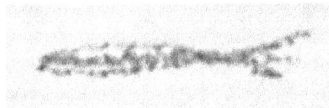

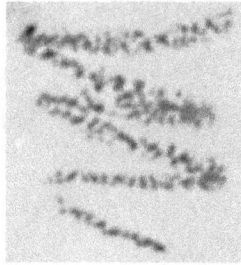

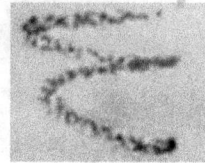

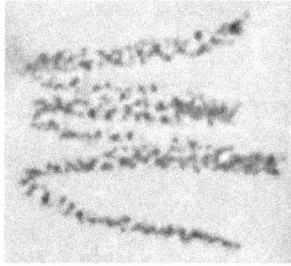

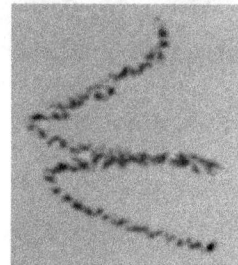

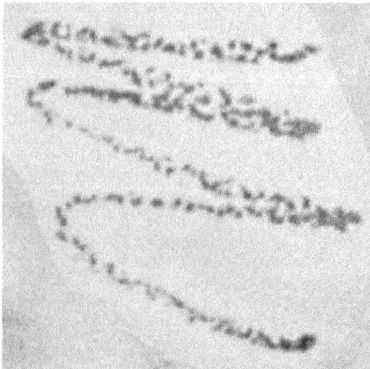

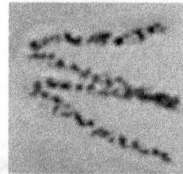

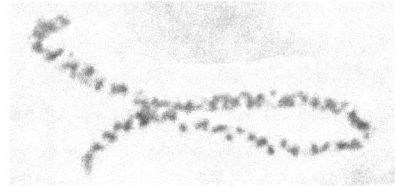

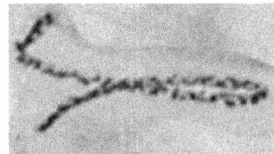

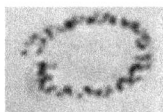

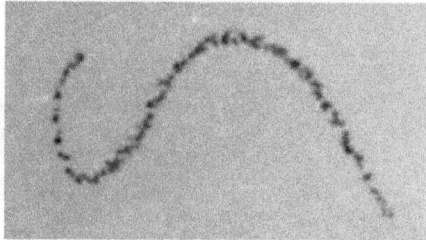

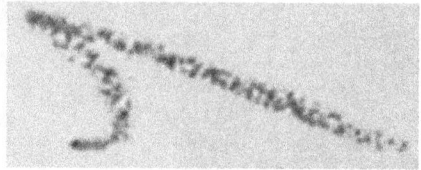

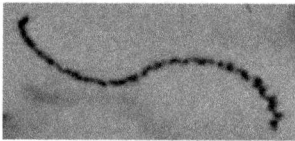

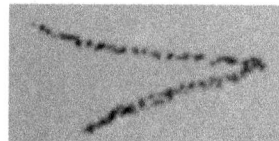

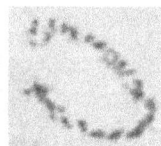

APPENDIX

LIPSTICK KILLER WALL CODE
DECRYPTION

WORD LIST

Notes: (this page intentionally left blank)

LIPSTICK KILLER WALL CODE / WORD FREQUENCY LIST

1	=		
2	=		
3	=		
4	=		
5	=		
6	S	1	**1 S T**
7	=		**A**
8	=		**A**
9	=		**A**
10	=		**A**
11	=		**A**
12			

1 1 1 1 1 = **A A A A A**

Initial for "Alice" =

A B H O R R E N C E

ADVICE

AFFIRM

ALIBI

ALL

AM AM

AND ARE ARE ARE ARE AS AS

= = = = = = = = = = = =

13 14 15 16 17 18 19 20 21 22 23 24 25 26

AS AT AT BACK BE BE BE BE BEAR BECAUSE BEEN BEFORE BELIEVE BRIEF

=

27
28
29
30
31
32
33
34
35
36
37
38
39
40

phonetic spelling for "Brown"

abbreviation for "California"

BRIEF

BROWN

CALIFORNIA

CAME

CAN

CAN

CAN

CANNOT

CAREFULLY

CATCH

CATCH

BY

BY

CA

= = = = = = = = = = = = = = = =

41
42
43
44
45
46
47
48
49
50
51
52
53
54

CLEARLY

COMBINED

=

COME

=

CONCLUSION

=

CONTROL

=

CRIME

=

CONTROVERSY

CONTROL

=

DO DO

=   =

DONE   EACH

=

=   =

ENJOYMENT

=

EVIL EVIL

=   =

55 56 57 58 59 60 61 62 63 64 65 66 67 68

FACTS FALSE

FINISHED

FINAL

EVIL EVIL FACTS FALSE FAME FEAR FEAR FEEL FEEL FEEL FEEL FEEL FINAL FINISHED

= = = = = = = = = = = = = =

69 70 71 72 73 74 75 76 77 78 79 80 81 82

proper noun

proper noun

city

FIRM

F L O V A

F O O L

F O O R

F O O R

F O O R

F O O R

F O O R

F O U R

F O U R

F O U R T E E N

F R A N C E S

F R A N C I S C O

F R O M

=

83
84
85
86
87
88
89
90
91
92
93
94
95
96

FROM FROM FROM FROM FROM FROM FROM HAVE HE HEAD HEAVENS HELL HELL HER

= = = = = = = = = = = = = =

97 98 99 100 101 102 103 104 105 106 107 108 109 110

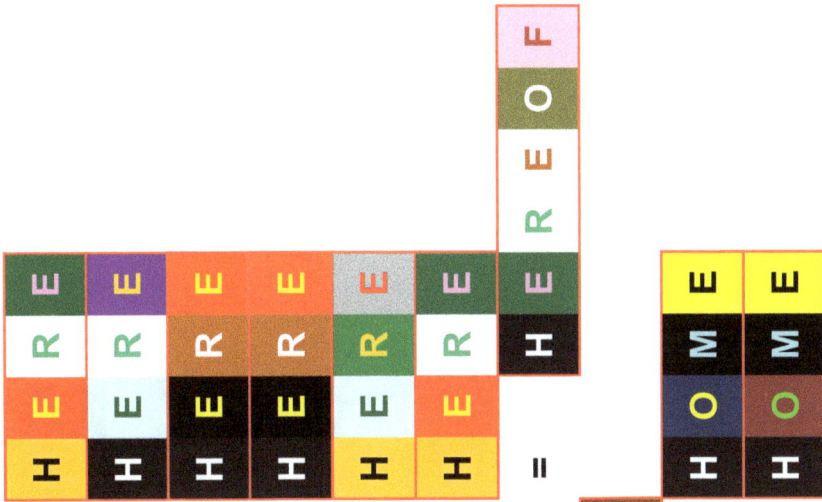

111
112
113
114
115
116
117
118
119
120
121
122
123
124

abbreviation for Illinois

contraction I"ll

contraction I"ll

contraction I"ll

contraction I'm

contraction I'm

I M	I M	I N	I N	I N	I N	I N	I S	I S	I S	I S	I S

J A C K		
J A C K		

= = = = = = = = = = = =

= =

139

140

141

142

143

144

145

146

147

148

149

150

151

152

phonetic
spelling for
"Josephine"

JACK = JOB = ... KILL = KILLER = KNIFE = LAST = LATER = LEARN = LEARN = LINE = LOOK = LOOK

JOSEFINE

153   154   155   156   157   158   159   160   161   162   163   164   165   166

MADE MAKE MAKE MAKE MAKE

MAN

ME ME ME ME ME ME ME ME

= = = = =

=

= = = = = = = =

167 168 169 170 171 172 173 174 175 176 177 178 179 180

MERE = MERE = MORE = MORE = MOTHER =

MR = MR = MS = MY = MY = MY = MY = MY =

MYSELF =

181 182 183 184 185 186 187 188 189 190 191 192 193 194

195 NAME

196 NAME

197 NAVY

198 YEAR

199 NECK

200 NEVER =

201 NINE

202 NINE

203

204 NOON

205 NOON

206 NOT

207 NOT

208 NOT

NOTES NOTES NOTES NOTES NOTES NUMBER

OFF OFF OFF OFF OFF OFF

= = = = = = = = = = = = =

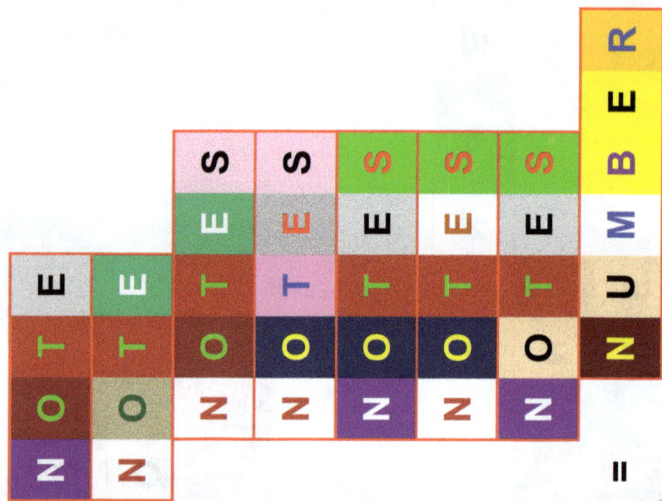

209 210 211 212 213 214 215 216 217 218 219 220 221 222

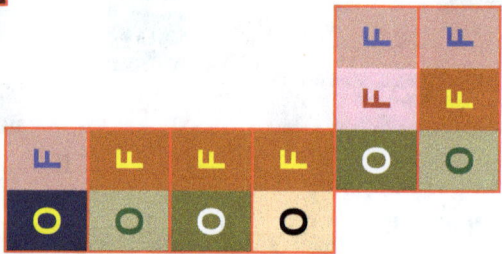

OFF

OFTEN

OLE

ON

NO

ONE

OVERALL

RANK

READ

REAL

REALLY

REASON

REFERENCE

223
224
225
226
227
228
229
230
231
232
233
234
235
236

REMEMBER

slang for "residence"

REVELS   REVELS

RHYME   RHYME   RHYME

RISE

ROSS

proper noun

naval rank

C

proper noun

= RES = R

= RISE

= ROSS

1   SAKE

SAKE   SAN

SEE   SEE   SEE

237
238
239
240
241
242
243
244
245
246
247
248
249
250

251

252

253

254

255

256

257

258

259

260

261

262

263

264

SEE =

SEE =

SEVENTEEN = SEVEN

SEVERAL = SEVERAL

SF = abbreviation for San Francisco

SHAME = SHAME

SHOT = SHOT

SHIER = SHIER

SMALL = SMALL

SMARTER = SMARTER

SO = SO

SO = SO

SOME = SOME

SORRY = SORRY

proper noun

SURNAME TALES TARRANCE TARRANCES

THAT THE THE THE THE THEM THERE THERE THERE

265 265 266 267 268 269 270 271 272 273 274 275 276 277

THERE

THREE

THRICE

=

=

=

TO OOOO TO

=

TRACK

USED

VEIL

VERSE

VICTIM

VICTIM

=

=

=

=

=

=

=

=

=

278

279

280

281

282

283

284

285

286

287

288

289

290

291

292 293 294 295

Notes: (this page intentionally left blank)

Notes: (this page intentionally left blank)